Great Lodges
OF THE WEST

By Christine Barnes

Photography by Fred Pflughoft & David Morris

Title Page: Soaring "head house" lobby, Timberline Lodge, Mt. Hood National Forest, Oregon
Above: El Tovar washed by the setting sun, Grand Canyon National Park, Arizona.

To
My mother and my stepfather,
Beverly and "Duke" Wellington,
who continue to discover the West
and
My father,
Bradley J. Hurd,
who built his own "Great Lodge"

Acknowledgments

The curators, historical architects, archivists, historians, and National Park Service and U.S. Forest Service personnel and volunteers, who shared their expertise. Linny Adamson, Sarah Allaback, Kim Besom, Richard Bartlett, Kevin Brandt, Janene Caywood, Gordon Chappell, Reid Coen, Laurin C. Huffman, Bob Jacobs, Victoria Jacobson, Jeff Jaqua, Stephen Mark, George Mason, Kirby Matthew, Henry Matthews, Jim McDonald, Sarah Munro, Paul Newman, Kelly Shakespear, Deirdre Shaw, Jim Snyder, David Wark, Lee and Tamela Whittlesey, W.B. Yeo, to name a few.

Also AmFac, Inc., Crater Lake Company, Glacier Park, Inc., Mt. Rainier Guest Services, Oregon Caves Company, RLK Company, Yosemite Concession Services Corp., especially Bob Baker, Barry Cantor, Jane Gillespie, Richard Kohnstamm, Kathleen McElfresh, Lu MacCarter, Ryan Oland, Michael Romick, Dale Scott, James Sproatt, Dennis Standish, Keith Walklet, and Cindy Wilson.

A special thanks to Don Compton for believing in the project, Tessie Bundick for her research assistance, Deborah Bourke for her friendship and support. And always, Jerry, Melissa and Michael.

Seventh Printing

Design & Illustration by Linda McCray
Edited by Teresa Record

Publisher's Cataloging-in-Publication Data
(prepared by Quality Books, Inc.)

Barnes, Christine, 1947-
   Great lodges of the West / Christine Barnes ;
photographs by
Fred Pflughoft and David Morris.
   p. cm.
   Includes bibliographical reference and Index.
   ISBN 0-9653924-1-4

   1. National parks and reserves--West (U.S.)--
Buildings. 2.
Hotels--West (U.S.)--Guidebooks. 3. Historic
buildings--West
(U.S.) 4. Resort architecture--West (U.S.) I. Title

TX907.B37 1997   647.9478'01
                                 QBI97-40074

Library of Congress catalog card number 97-60024

Printed in Hong Kong by C&C Offset Printing Co., LTD.

Many Glacier Hotel cupped in glaciated grandeur, Glacier National Park, Montana.

Contents

President Franklin D. Roosevelt dedicates Timberline Lodge, a WPA project in the Mt. Hood National Forest, September 28, 1937.

National Trust for Historic Preservation

1785 Massachusetts Avenue, N.W.
Washington, D.C. 20036
(202) 588-6105

Richard Moe
President

FOREWORD

The National Parks of the West are among America's greatest treasures. *Great Lodges of the West* reminds us that these scenic wonderlands, best known for their mountains, canyons, geysers and waterfalls, are also dotted with the brick-and-board evidence of our nation's history.

Glacier National Park, to cite a single example, is home to more than 300 historic structures. Many of them are in serious peril. The Sperry and Granite Park chalets, built early in this century to provide a unique visitor experience in Glacier's remote backcountry, have been closed to the public since 1992 out of concern for environmental and visitor safety. The famous Many Glacier Hotel, featured in this book, is still in service at present—but it could share the same fate in the near future unless extensive structural repairs are made. The cost of restoring these three buildings alone is estimated in the millions of dollars.

Glacier represents only the tip of the iceberg. In the western United States the National Park Service (NPS) is responsible for 5,000 historic structures in its sprawling region—yet the Region's annual preservation budget is a grossly inadequate $1.5 million. Nationwide, NPS has been entrusted with responsibility for over 20,000 historic structures. Despite a generally praiseworthy record of good stewardship over the years, the agency currently faces a multimillion dollar backlog in rehabilitation and restoration of historic structures and cultural landscapes, and millions more are needed for scheduled inspections, stabilization and maintenance. These numbers translate into a bleak reality: Historic structures are not receiving adequate maintenance—and once they begin to fail, funds for repair and restoration are too often unavailable.

The President and Congress are considering a variety of ways—ranging from raising entrance fees to forging partnerships with private-sector individuals and the business community—to bring new capital into the parks. Whatever funding mechanisms are employed, it is imperative that the needs of historic resources be addressed on an equal footing with demands for natural resource protection, rail maintenance and wildlife habitat. What is needed is a dedicated fund for maintenance of historic structures in the national park system.

Now, before it's too late, is the time for all of us to let it be known that the cultural heritage embodied in our National Parks is worth whatever it takes to save it. To lose these buildings is to lose a part of the American soul.

RICHARD MOE
President
National Trust for Historic Preservation

Carpenters gather in front of Old Faithful Inn, Yellowstone National Park, 1904.

Introduction

Great Lodges of the West began as a simple weekend trip to Oregon's "new" Crater Lake Lodge. It ended with this volume covering twelve of the best examples of the West's "wilderness" architecture. Eight lodges are in National Parks, one in a National Monument, one in a National Forest, one on ceded Indian reservation land, and one across the U.S. border in Parks Canada—they are all national treasures.

The lodges were selected for their historic and architectural significance with the guidance of National Park Service (NPS) historical architects. As my research and travel evolved, two things stood out. First, that the National Parks and the National Park Service happened at all seems miraculous, and second, that even under the worst of circumstances, architects, building and railroad crews, masons and carpenters, landscape designers, businessmen and local boosters never gave up. Structures collapsed during winter storms, roads turned into bogs as wagons loaded with supplies sank into the mud; wind blew buildings out of plumb; financing vanished and the desolate locations made every ordinary phase of construction an obstacle.

Yet, when completed, the lodges were beyond shelters; they were monuments to the wilds of the West and the perseverance of the men and women who created them. Each lodge holds stories nailed in every board foot, dreams secured in stone and mortar and memories found in hand-carved details.

Important people such as Stephen T. Mather, the first director of the National Park Service; Horace Albright, his assistant, who also became director; Frederick Law Olmsted, Jr., a member of the Commission of Fine Arts and noted landscape architect; Daniel Hull and Thomas Vint, NPS landscape architects; dozens of politicians, including presidents Theodore Roosevelt, Herbert Hoover and Franklin D. Roosevelt; and railroad barons like Louis Hill and E.P. Ripley all played important roles. But it was the men who took pencil to paper and drew plans for the lodges who deserve the real credit. Some became quite famous, others faded into obscurity, but most went on to careers that included designing hotels, theaters, train depots and homes. Much of their work was lost to fire or "progress," felled by wrecking ball and bulldozer.

The stylistic roots of these lodges are credited to the English Arts and Crafts Movement, first seen in the U.S. in the great camps of the Adirondacks. At the turn of the 20th century, Americans, urbanized and inundated with Victorian excess, latched onto the idea of simple, utilitarian, hand-crafted homes and furnishings. The Craftsman magazine, edited by Gustav Stickley, a designer, philosopher and social critic, promoted the idea of this architectural and social reform. Those who designed the Great Lodges drew from the Shingle, Prairie and Mission styles, often with a heavy dose of European alpine chalet design. What evolved over three decades was an all American interpretation. The overriding premise was that the buildings must blend with the landscape, be part of the environment.

Supplemented by wilderness literature of the era, and a desire to recapture their pioneer roots, the public was longing to discover the "West" from Canada to Mexico and as far as the Pacific Ocean. When they arrived—on trains, stagecoaches and (later) automobiles—the often rustic rock and timber structures offered perfect shelter.

The National Park Service, established in 1916, was instrumental in creating an architectural vernacular of rustic design, often referred to as "parkitecture," that flourished until the mid-1930s. The romanticism of rustic architecture fell victim to changing times, materials and design philosophies. Considered by some to be a drain on resources and maintenance staffs, many of these aging lodges were recommended for demolition. Happily for the millions of visitors who step into each lobby, and hence into the past, these lodges still survive.

The architecture and engineering of each lodge featured in Great Lodges of the West is spectacular. Yet, it is the detail—the forged ironwork, notched and joined massive timbers, stonework and handmade furniture—that makes these lodges part of our history. Some suffer from the ravages of winter climates and may be a bit threadbare, but the grandeur of each building overshadows the tracks of time.

Old Faithful Geyser and its namesake Inn stand as natural and cultural landmarks in Yellowstone, America's first National Park. Jeff and Alexa Henry

Old Faithful Inn

First of the Great Western Lodges

There is a sense of frenzy at Yellowstone National Park. Each year three million visitors, high on the anticipation of encountering bison, bear, elk, moose, coyote and wolves, visit America's first National Park. The wildlife roam 2.2 million acres of mountainous, deeply gorged, fire-scarred, geyser-studded landscape interspersed with gentle meadows and meandering rivers. It all seems beyond this world. By the time visitors focus their attention on Old Faithful Geyser, their adrenaline is pumped as high as the plumes of steam and scalding water that spew like clockwork from the earth. Then they turn to Old Faithful Inn.

And that is how architect Robert Reamer wanted it. Old Faithful Inn does not face its namesake. Visitors approach the Inn with eyes fixed on the geyser, the building to the side. While Old Faithful Inn is a structural wonder, the real brilliance is Reamer's understanding of the power of its setting. Even in 1902, when this relatively unknown architect began designing the Inn, he understood the draw of nature. He let the landscape not only introduce his creation, but he used the rough-and-tumble ingredients of the region from which to build it.

That region was established as the first National Park by an Act of Congress on March 1, 1872, and its management was put under the Secretary of the Interior. His responsibility was twofold:

to protect the miraculous, seemingly sacred swath of land and to make it accessible to the public. It was a difficult task, and by 1886, the U.S. Army was put in charge to control the souvenir-hunters, poachers and bandits who had a very different definition of "sacred." Almost as difficult was granting leases for construction of accommodations. Visitors arrived by rail at one of two entrances to the park and transferred to horse-drawn "tally-ho" stagecoaches to continue their journey.

Early park accommodations were primitive tent compounds. From 1883 to 1891, the Yellowstone Park Association, a subsidiary of the Northern Pacific Railway, built hotels along Yellowstone's grand loop roads. But visitors, not content with a side trip to Old Faithful Geyser, wanted a place to spend the night within the wildly exotic Upper Geyser Basin. In 1885, the first hotel, a ramshackle building dubbed "the shack," was built. It burned

in 1894, and an equally ramshackle wood building was constructed in its place. In 1899, the acting park superintendent noted in his annual report that the "system of hotels should include one at the Upper Geyser Basin.... An opportunity to see some of the greatest geysers in action is often lost to tourists by their not being able to stay over night here."

All the while, mismanagement and financial woes plagued the companies attempting to run the facilities. The Northern Pacific, interested in securing its position at the park, eventually bought majority stock in the Yellowstone Park Association (earlier YPIC). In the spring of 1901, the railroad sold its controlling stock in the Yellowstone Park Association to Harry Child, Edmund Bach and Silas Huntley, owners of the Yellowstone Transportation Company, with the hope that the new owners would work with the railroad to bring tourists to the park via the Northern Pacific line. Child was soon named president of the association and became a powerful force at Yellowstone and in Washington, D.C.

During this time, the subject of a hotel at the Upper Geyser Basin was an ongoing point of contention. Park regulations required structures to be one-quarter mile from a natural object of interest—officials of the Yellowstone Park Association wanted the new hotel to be closer to Old Faithful

LOCATION: Yellowstone National Park, Wyoming

OPENED: June 1904

ARCHITECT: Robert C. Reamer

HISTORIC DESIGNATION: National Historic Landmark, May 28, 1987

Geyser. In 1894, a new regulation allowed building one-eighth mile from the geyser. Still, it was four years before an architect designed a hotel for the site. The Department of the Interior approved A.W. Spalding's plans for a Queen Anne style hotel, but nothing happened. By 1900, frustrated Department of Interior officials were pressing for construction of a hotel.

But it was not A.W. Spalding's vision that became reality next to the most famous geyser in Yellowstone National Park. Instead, Child hired Robert Reamer to design what would become the first Great Lodge of the West. An Ohio native and self-taught architect, Reamer worked early on for a Chicago architectural firm and was a partner in his own San Diego firm, where he likely met Child.

Old Faithful Inn became the model for lodge design in the West; it reflects the same philosophy espoused by the Arts and Crafts Movement being embraced at that time in America. Simplicity, use of native materials, handwork and blending of the building with the site were the movement's fundamental principles. Reamer was true to that philosophy at Old Faithful Inn, but his work is varied. In 1911, he went to work for the New York, New Haven and Hartford Railroad, and later he settled in Seattle, where he built a reputation on hotel and theater designs that included Chinese, Art Deco and Spanish/Moorish. Perhaps his penchant for theater design first appeared at Old Faithful Inn. The lodge, rooted in the landscape, also has an element of high drama.

A massive gable roof dominates the original portion of the Inn, which is called the Old House.

The six-story, steeply pitched roof offers the immediate feeling of shelter, but its shape is that of a big-top tent, a feeling reinforced by the flag poles that line the widow's walk built along the peak. Originally, guests climbed through the lobby stairway and the suspended balconies, through the crow's nest and onto the roof for a 360-degree view of the Upper Geyser Basin. A spotlight on the widow's walk pointed out erupting geysers and prowling bears, much like a ringmaster highlighting circus acts. "A geyser seen in eruption under the searchlight is a most remarkable sight," a 1905 Northern Pacific Railway brochure exclaimed. A second light was added, but both were removed in 1948; the widow's walk was closed to the public in 1959.

Below the widow's walk, Reamer placed a series of dormer windows that not only break the

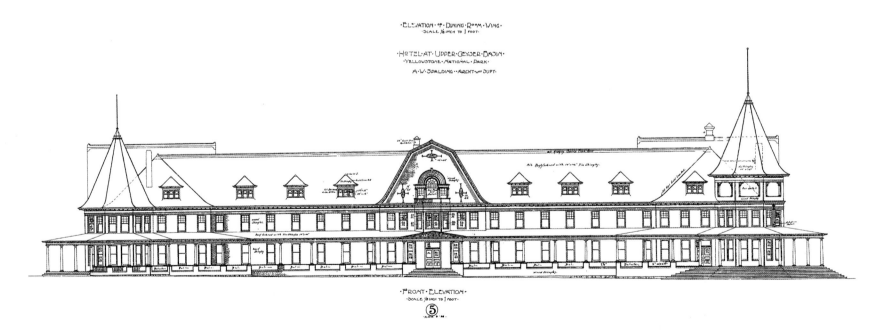

severe roofline, but provide filtered light into the great hall. Hand-hewn logs cover the lower exterior, while cedar shingles cover the upper floors. The Inn's masonry foundation is of stone quarried nearby. Huge cribbed-log piers support the porte-cochère and the veranda that rests above it.

The Inn may be part of Yellowstone's supporting cast, but entering the lodge under the overhang, through the massive red doors and into the great-hall lobby puts visitors on center stage. The ceiling rises eighty-five feet, and the series of balconies and hanging stairways through the log columns and gnarled supports gives the distinct feeling of being in a tree house. A crow's nest built in the upper reaches of the ceiling gave access to the widow's walk. It also provided a venue for musicians who climbed to the crow's nest after the

dinner performance. Their climb may have entertained the guests as much as the post-dinner music they provided from above.

Light filters into the great hall through a variety of square, round, diamond and elliptical window panes, then the trunks and branches of the interior supports, much like a natural forest. Reamer left the bark on the logs; it was peeled for easier maintenance while the lodge was closed during World War II. Still, the essence of a forest setting survives, in large part due to the gnarled lodgepole-pine decorative supports and balustrades that line the mezzanine and balconies. These decorative elements say volumes about Reamer's sense of style and fun. The gnarled logs and limbs are a contrast to the serious business of creating a structure that could withstand twenty-foot drifts of

Opposite: A.W. Spalding's original Queen Anne design was approved by the Department of the Interior, but never constructed—a decision that helped define Western park architecture.

Below: Instead, Robert Reamer was commissioned for the job. Drawings of his rustic design illustrate the asymmetrical details so in keeping with the strangely magnificent setting.

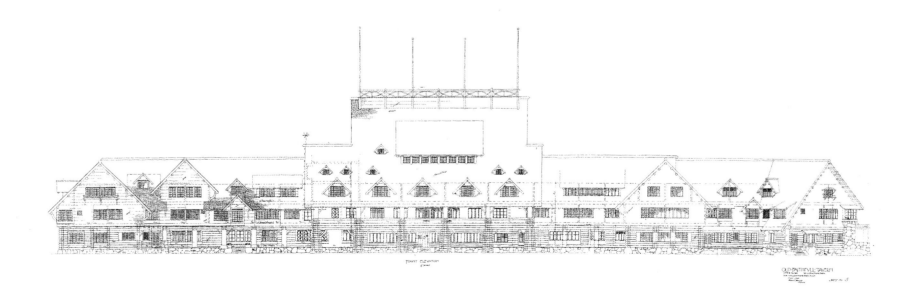

Above: Stairways of split logs and gnarled lodgepole pine connect the Inn's great hall and mezzanines.

Opposite: The lava-rock fireplace rises through the eighty-five-foot ceiling of the Inn's great hall. Besides the Inn, deemed a masterpiece, architect Robert Reamer designed the clock and candlelight fixtures.

snow and temperatures that could dip to sixty degrees below zero.

If the gnarled lodgepole pieces seem frivolous, the massive fireplace, built of 500 tons of lava rock and placed on a sixteen-foot base, is a serious anchor for the room. Tapering to a modified pyramid, it dominates the great hall with four large hearths and four smaller ones in each corner.

Hanging from the fireplace is a huge windup clock designed by Reamer. He also designed the imitation candlestick light fixtures that circle the log columns, copper light fixtures and some of the furniture—all in the Arts and Crafts motif.

Guests enter the dining room, behind the lobby, through heavy double doors hung from the same kind of iron hinges found on the main entry. Workers forged this ironwork and other pieces on site. The room feels like a huge, traditional log cabin, with split logs covering the open, pitched roof and walls. Scissor log trusses support the roof with gusset plate and iron rod supports.

The stone fireplace on the south dining room wall collapsed in 1959 during the 7.5 earthquake. It was rebuilt to its original design and completed in 1989 with a historical blacksmith re-creating the fire-screen. The dining room fireplace and the brick portion of the chimney in the great hall were the only two notable victims of that quake or the almost indiscernible ones that rumble through the park daily.

Large windows flanked each side of the fireplace; they were converted to doors when the second dining room was added. Formally attired diners ate family-style at long tables when the Inn first opened. The reed dining-room chairs are original; the bats that sweep through the room on warm late-summer nights are not.

Opposite: In 1915, the first automobile arrived at the Inn on the rutted dirt roads used by horse-drawn "tally-ho" stagecoaches.

Left: Spectacular sights, including the hourly eruption of Old Faithful Geyser, can be seen from the veranda above the porte-cochère.

Above: Bedrooms in the "Old House" retain their original charm.

17

The original Old House had 140 rooms. Most of the guest rooms were down hallways off the east and west sides of the lobby. The first-floor rooms, with communal baths, featured rustic log decor, while the rooms on the floors above were finished with rough, unpainted pine boards. Only ten rooms had private baths. Today, there are eighty-three rooms in the Old House, changed little over time except for the addition of sinks. By the time the Old House was complete, Child had spent nearly $140,000 of the railway's money on the building and another $25,000 on the furnishings.

Those furnishings were predominately Mission-style tables, davenports, rockers and settees, with rustic hickory tables and chairs in the lobby and mezzanine. Oak double-writing desks with high spindle dividers and art glass center shades offered the perfect place for visitors to make journal entries or write letters about the wonders of what was just outside the door. Guest-room furnishings included iron or wood beds, green finished dressers, chairs and night-stands, desks, chamber pots and wash-stands.

Today, the Inn still has a number of original pieces or pieces salvaged from the Canyon Hotel before its scheduled demolition in the 1950s. The Limbert chairs in the south dining room and some of the reading desks on the mezzanine are from the Canyon Hotel.

The Inn was an immediate success with the traveling public. Reamer designed and supervised the construction of the east wing addition in 1913-14, adding one hundred guest rooms at about $1,000 each. The flat tar-and-gravel roof with a mansard overhang gave little competition to the

Old House and its spectacular pitched roof. Cedar shingles covered the exterior walls, but the interior offered a very different atmosphere. Plaster, not wood, covered the walls. The furnishings were simple and rather austere.

In 1927, Reamer designed a west wing addition with 150 rooms and 95 bathrooms at a cost of over $200,000. It was not a pleasant experience.

Carousing bears and a curious pelican depicted in glass etchings.

Since the building of the Inn and first wing, the National Park Service (NPS) had been established and with it a Landscape Engineering Division that became involved. A flurry of correspondence ensued among Reamer, park supervisor Horace Albright and Harry Child, with opinions from other government officials. The new wing would be more visible than the 1913 addition, and Reamer wanted it to be a flat-roof design so as not to

compete with the Old House. The Park Service vehemently objected to the roof design, and Albright wrote Child that the addition was "...so different from the old building that it was bound to be commented on adversely." Reamer responded in a telegram to Child, "[I] am just as much interested in not marring the appearance of Old Faithful as the government and as I designed the old building and wasn't shot for it I according to the code of ethics feel I should be trusted to finish the designing."

Finally, as a 200-man crew began construction, government and park officials approved the original plan with a flat roof, mansard overhang and dormer windows. A fourth story was added to accommodate additional bathrooms.

Dining room additions came more easily and in phases, beginning in 1920 with a temporary canvas-roofed addition to the south of the main dining room. The permanent log structure was completed for the 1922 season. Inside, a more sophisticated atmosphere replaces the log cabin feel of the main dining room. Interior columns and beams, etched with designs and pictures of park wildlife, bring a refined touch of the outdoors inside. In 1927, another room was attached to the side of the main dining room. This multisided room is now the Bear Pit cocktail lounge.

The lobby was reconfigured as needs of the Inn evolved. The sunken lounge around the fireplace, cordoned off by log railings, created an element of seclusion in the midst of much activity. In 1927, the ground-floor front wall was moved forward beneath the porte-cochère to create space for an enlarged gift shop. The new space also

"afforded more dancing room" and the sunken, railed fireplace lounge was filled and made part of the great hall. Earlier, guest rooms were removed around the lobby to make space for an art shop, bellhops' desk, new registration desk and store.

One of Reamer's last projects at Old Faithful Inn left a legacy to the architect's sense of humor. The original Bear Pit Lounge was created in 1936, in part, to celebrate the repeal of prohibition in 1933 and the NPS's 1934 decision to allow the sale of alcoholic drinks in the parks. The room, now the snack bar tucked between the kitchen and west wing of the Old House, was lined with vertical-grain fir veneer. Reamer wanted some of the panels decorated with sand blast designs. He wrote in an October 18, 1934, memo to the president of the Yellowstone Park Hotel Company, "I wouldn't mind adding a touch of humor to this room. If your Chicago cartoonist would rough out some of his funny bears they might be used to advantage."

The result was twelve panels of dancing, hard-drinking, card-playing, party bears along with their more refined bruins. A pair of ballroom dancing moose and a ram waiter add to the hilarious lineup. A successful park advertising campaign featured the bears minus libation. Today, some of the original wood panels are in the snack bar behind protective glass. In 1988, artists reproduced the panels in glass etchings that divide the main dining room wall and cocktail lounge.

During the decade that Reamer worked for Child, he designed many of the major buildings either within the park or nearby in Montana. In 1902, he designed both Old Faithful Inn and the log depot in Gardiner, Montana. Other architectural achievements included the second Canyon Hotel, built in 1911 (slated for demolition in 1959, but mysteriously burned in 1960), and extensive

changes to the Lake Hotel that turned it from a boxy building into a neoclassical hotel. He also submitted plans for Mammoth Springs Hotel in 1909 (some were used and others never executed) and the cottages behind that hotel. In 1925, he designed four residences at Gardiner for the Yellowstone Transportation Co., plus a number of small buildings.

Reamer became close friends with Mr. and Mrs. Harry Child, and as his daughter, Jane Reamer White, noted in 1970 correspondence, "What does seem certain is that Mr. and Mrs. Child took quite a personal interest in my father, right from the start. For extended periods during construction in the Park, he resided in their home." Reamer was also included in a 1909 European trip with the Childs, giving the young, still-single architect the opportunity of seeing "…the famous architectural achievements abroad." Mr. and Mrs. Child admired his work enough to have him design their private residence.

In 1988, Robert Reamer's greatest remaining park achievement, Old Faithful Inn, was nearly lost when Yellowstone's most treacherous fire roared towards the structure. Burning embers arrived five miles ahead of the flames. An exterior sprinkler system, installed the year before, drenched the roof of the Old House and volunteers beat flames from the flat roofs of the wings and hosed them with water. The wind changed, and the Inn was saved.

Old Faithful Inn is under a constant state of maintenance. In the early 1980s, major work began that included fire-safety improvements, electrical upgrades and gutting of the kitchen. The NPS architects completed renovation work of the back lobby entrance, gift shop, service desks and dining rooms in 1988.

The Inn is operated by TW Recreational Services, Inc. TWRS, a subsidiary of AmFac Parks and Resorts, Inc., is authorized to provide concession services in Yellowstone. The contract requires that TWRS invest ten percent of its annual gross revenue into a Capital Improvement Program and ten percent into a Cyclic Maintenance Program for the government-owned facilities assigned to TWRS for its park operations. In addition, the contract called for TWRS to advance $8 million during the first three years of the contract for a park construction and improvement program. As a result, in 1992, $6 million was spent on renovating eighty-three guest rooms and public areas in the east and west wings of the Inn.

A&E Architects and River Run Interiors from Billings, Montana, in conjunction with the National Park Service and TWRS, transformed the austere guest rooms into charming rooms with full, modern bathrooms while still keeping the original sense of the place. The craftsman-style maple and wicker furnishing are faithful to the era in which the wings were built.

During renovation, the east wing was taken down to its skeleton on the inside, updated and returned to be an improved version of its original self. Some fixtures and hardware were reused, and the trimwork in the hallways, the texturing of sheet rock, and the colors were all selected based on historical records. Soft yellow, cream, rust and light green never overpower the decor. Since then, a historic preservation crew of five to six people with special craft skills, trained on site with the Park Service, takes on restoration projects.

Old Faithful Inn was the first and some feel the finest Great Lodge of the West. Like many of these lodges, the Inn has become more than a hostelry, a not-to-be-missed stop on the incredible journey through Yellowstone National Park.

"Old Faithful Inn is almost as great an attraction for Yellowstone Park as the wonderful geyser phenomena or the profound Gran Cañon," stated a 1905 Northern Pacific brochure.

The Santa Fe Railway wanted both elegance and rusticity in El Tovar. Charles Whittlesey delivered by merging log cabin and European villa designs.

Grande Dame of the South Rim

If Robert Reamer designed Old Faithful Inn to pay homage to Old Faithful Geyser, it was a given that architect Charles Whittlesey's El Tovar Hotel should not attempt to compete with its extraordinary environment. Yellowstone National Park is a barrage of natural wonders. The Grand Canyon itself is simply a heart-stopper.

Even with the overpowering impact of the canyon, the Illinois architect, trained in the Chicago office of Louis Sullivan, rose to the occasion. As an architect for the Atchison, Topeka & Santa Fe Railway designing hotels and stations on the line, Whittlesey saw an opportunity to meld the elegance of a European villa with an American hunting lodge. Whittlesey cut his Southwestern teeth in 1901 when he designed the Mission-style Alvarado Hotel and railway depot, both in Albuquerque, New Mexico. While working for the Santa Fe, Whittlesey made his headquarters in Albuquerque, where he designed his own home after finishing El Tovar plans. A three-story log structure with a low-pitched roof, and a wide porch, in many ways, his home is a smaller version of his famous hotel. And why not? El Tovar is as elegant and warm as it is eclectic.

Dubbed Bright Angel Tavern during the planning stages, the name was changed before its opening to the more suitable El Tovar Hotel, in keeping with the Santa Fe's tradition of naming its

hotels of the region after Spanish explorers. Pedro de Tobar never actually got to the South Rim of the canyon with the 1540 Francisco Vásquez de Coronado expedition. No matter, the "b" in his name was changed to a "v" (the antique Spanish spelling also

eliminated the possible mispronunciation of "to-the-bar" that the Santa Fe feared), and the grand hotel was officially named.

Like other railways at the turn of the 20th century, the Atchison, Topeka & Santa Fe was opening up tourism in exotic American landscapes. By 1901, when the railway completed a branch from its

Chicago-Los Angeles main line to the South Rim of the Grand Canyon, prospectors had staked numerous claims. Potential income from the budding tourist trade seemed more profitable than mining ore, and prospectors quickly adapted. This colorful lot built trails (charging a use toll) and became outfitters, guides and innkeepers. Small hotels and cabins, serviced by stage lines, were the first tourist accommodations. Early tourists stayed at the Grandview Hotel, built in 1895 eleven miles east of the South Rim, and Bright Angel Hotel and tent camp built soon after on the South Rim.

Explorers, geologists and others such as naturalist/conservationist John Muir and naturalist John Burroughs were all drawn to the "divine abyss," as Burroughs described the canyon. President Benjamin Harrison proclaimed the Grand Canyon Forest Reserve in 1893. But it was President Theodore Roosevelt's 1903 visit to the Grand Canyon that gave the American people an idea of just what that huge chasm in the seemingly barren high desert of Arizona was all about: "In the Grand Canyon, Arizona has a natural wonder which, so far as I know, is in kind absolutely unparalleled throughout the rest of the world. I want to ask you to do one thing in connection with it in your own interest and in the interest of the country—to keep this great wonder of nature as it is now.... I hope

LOCATION: Grand Canyon National Park, Arizona
OPENED: January 14, 1905
ARCHITECT: Charles Whittlesey
HISTORIC DESIGNATION: National Historic Landmark, May 28, 1987

Below: An architectural drawing of the east entrance, done in 1983 as part of a major renovation, illustrates the variety of Charles Whittlesey's original design. The various numbers pinpoint proposed exterior repairs.

Right: Little has changed except the bellboys at the front desk and switchboard, 1905.

EAST ELEVATION

you will not have a building of any kind, not a summer cottage, a hotel or anything else, to mar the wonderful grandeur, the sublimity, the great loveliness and beauty of the Canyon. Leave it as it is. You cannot improve on it."

That was not the case. Roosevelt continued to support preservation of the Grand Canyon from Washington. In 1906, he created the Grand Canyon Game Reserve by executive order. That same year, he signed the Antiquities Act, which gave him legislative authority to establish Grand Canyon National Monument two years later. He also enlarged the Forest Reserve into a National Forest, although Arizona did not become a state until 1912. By the time the Grand Canyon became a National Park in 1919, the South Rim had already been developed, and El Tovar stood as the flagship of Grand Canyon Village. Along with railway development came the Fred Harvey Company, a hostelry and food service firm that had since the 1870s made itself a name for excellent service. With the creation of Grand Canyon National Park, Fred Harvey became the hotel, restaurant and gift shop concessionaire at the South Rim; its first South Rim contract was managing El Tovar.

Newspaper accounts and promotional material described the hotel as a combination of a "Swiss chateaux" and "castles of the Rhine." Even with its shingled-wrapped turret (water storage tank) and elegant interior solariums and lounges, it evoked the mood of the West that the Santa Fe was promoting. The railway spared no expense in building El Tovar. While Whittlesey used native boulders for the stunning foundation and rockwork, the huge Douglas-firs were shipped by rail from the Pacific Northwest. This pushed the cost of the hotel to $250,000, a huge sum, especially when compared to Old Faithful Inn, built for $140,000 in

1904. But potential profit for El Tovar was greater because the hotel could remain open all year.

In 1902, the Atchison Executive Committee authorized an advance of $75,000 to the Grand Canyon Railway, a subsidiary of the Atchison, Topeka & Santa Fe, to complete the building. "We were unable to have the work done in accordance with plans which covered a building of the character we desired and believed necessary, as cheaply as anticipated," railway president E.P. Ripley wrote to the chairman of the executive committee on September 19, 1904. "The hotel, when completed, however, will be first class in every particular, and unquestionably will be a money maker."

And it was. In 1909-10, the railway built the train station (designed by Santa Barbara architect Francis Wilson) just below the hotel. Guests arrived at the platform and looked up at the solariums, rooftop porches with ten-foot posts topped with trefoils, and the turret of El Tovar. From below, it appears very much the European castle. Yet, at the main entry, with its huge veranda supported by L-shaped, stone corner walls with arched openings, log columns, wide steps and gable roof with protruding log beams, it is a log cabin. El Tovar's architecture incorporates the very social transition of the era. Part Victorian resort and part rustic log cabin, it provided both the comforts of the known, established Eastern resorts and the excitement of the unknown West.

Every exterior view of the hotel produces just such a juxtaposition of style and design. Step back from the entry, and the long, low-slung feeling of the plan can be seen. The view from the rimside shows the log-slab sheathed dining, kitchen and utility wing, extending the cabin image, while gazebos off the north porch offer more refined shelter. A much-loved quote from C.A. Higgins' promo-

El Tovar's Rendezvous Room, 1905.

tional booklet *The Titan of Chasms* appears on the lintel above the porch: "Dreams of mountains, as in their sleep they brood on things eternal."

The location of the hotel and access to it by guests was meant as a buildup to the "surprise of the supreme moment," viewing the canyon itself. "The Hotel El Tovar stands near the rim.... It is not until the sightseer reaches the edge that the full force of the view strikes him with a shock that makes him gasp," exclaimed a 1905 Santa Fe Railway brochure.

No one gasps at the sight of El Tovar. National Park Service historians note that "...even with the eclectic design, thought was given to the relationship between the hotel and its setting. Such concern represented a distinct departure from strictly functional railroad architecture." Whittlesey stained the structure a dark brown, and when caught in the late day's sun, golden rays wash the building with

the same rich hues that bathe the canyon plummeting below. The massive hotel with its varied rooflines seems to sink into the landscape.

Unlike Reamer's "Wild West" Old Faithful Inn, Whittlesey turned to the Swiss jigsawn details for the balustrades on the porches, sun decks and interior stairways and balconies. He used the same pattern in his Albuquerque home, a detail later fancied by the Great Northern Railway architects in Glacier National Park.

Inside, El Tovar offers the same old-world charm with a heavy dose of rusticity. The main lobby, called the Rendezvous Room, is a hunting lodge personified. Dark-stained log-slab walls, heavy beams and rafters, a stone fireplace in the corner, and polished wood floors are the backdrop for the decor. "On the upper shelf repose heads of the deer, elk, moose, mountain sheep, and buffalo, mingling with curiously shaped, and gaudily-tinted

Part Victorian resort of the late 19th century and part rustic log cabin, El Tovar provided both the comforts of the established Eastern resorts and the excitement of the unknown West.

The Rotunda of El Tovar, "Where all paths intersect."

Indian jars from the Southwest pueblos," a 1909 brochure described the scene. The furniture was Arts and Crafts design, some later identified as Gustav Stickley. "Nothing cheap nor tawdry is tolerated," boasted the brochure. "No expense was spared in selecting the furniture." Much of the original furniture is gone, replaced in the 1970s with Mediterranean pieces, and the original Arts and Crafts light fixtures were replaced by copper chandeliers.

In 1995, the Rendezvous Room was redecorated to retain the room's original "retreat" atmosphere. Decorator Jeanne Crandall used a Navajo rug (shown in historical photos surrounded by rocking chairs by the fireplace) as a point of departure. She then incorporated its colors and design into the custom-loomed Axminster rug and upholstery fabric. The heavy wood sofas and chairs were also custom-made with the back and arm rails repeating the balustrade pattern from the main stairway. Many of the hunting trophies remain.

The registration lobby, or Rotunda, is where "all paths intersect." The log-fronted registration desk has changed little, and the mezzanine lounge above it has an octagonal balcony with jigsawn balustrade. This was the crimson-draped Ladies Lounge where "...the better half of the world may see without being seen—may chat and gossip—may sew and read—may do any of the inconsequent nothings which serve to pleasantly pass the time away." Ah, yes, the Victorian era.

Billiards, pool and cards were played in the ground-level Amusement Room; music and dancing were enjoyed in the ivory and gold trimmed Music Room with a view of the canyon; libation was taken by gentlemen in the Grotto; ladies "sun bathed" in the wicker filled Sun Parlor; and elegant meals, prepared by an "Italian chef, once employed in New York and Chicago clubs," were served in the eighty-nine-foot-long dining room, where the famed "Harvey girls" waited tables. A richly paneled, private dining room was (and still is) available for intimate dinners.

Most of the one hundred "sleeping rooms" were decorated with Arts and Crafts style furniture and painted Nile green, buff and cream. A dozen larger, more elaborate rooms featured colonial-design mahogany furniture with sleigh beds. Twenty-one bathrooms were "...white as snow and kept spotlessly clean." And lest we forget, "Steam heat, electric lights and office telephones are provided—willing servants quickly to do your bidding."

The Sun Parlor is now a guest suite, and in 1940, the Music Room was converted into four guest rooms. Redecorating of five "signature" suites was completed in 1995, each with an individual theme. Again, Crandall took an inventory of the existing and stored pieces and created rooms incorporating these treasures. While each suite is different—the former Sun Parlor is done in burgundy with a traditional four-poster bed and armoire, and the Painter's Suite, including an easel with painting, is furnished in Mission style—they all reflect the popular styles of the period.

There are now seventy-eight guest rooms, each with a private bath. What was the Amusement Room still has the rubble masonry walls with elegant arched openings that replicate the arches at the front of the building, but the pool and card tables have been replaced by public restrooms, phone banks and storage facilities. And today, even those who don't qualify as "ladies" can enjoy the mezzanine lounge. The lounge's crimson decor is gone, but the room is still charming with a corner fireplace and peeled log posts with decorative corbels supporting the beams.

In 1905, Arts and Crafts furniture and light fixtures decorated the dining room, left, and mahogany sleigh beds were featured in some of the bedroom suites, below.

Bottom: A full front view of El Tovar just after construction, 1904.

The 1979 remodeling of the dining room made it more elegant than the original design. The huge room (three times the size of the Rendezvous Room), has two stone chimneys, one on the north and one on the south, each flanked by large picture windows. Four large murals by Brue Himeche depict the customs of four Indian tribes: the Hopi, Apache, Mojave, and Navajo. The simple Arts and Crafts period chairs and tables were replaced with elegant armchairs. Stained-glass lights now hang instead of the original log chandeliers. A side porch was converted to the Canyon dining room, where a 1920 Chris Jorgenson painting hangs opposite the bank of windows facing the rim. Porches along the dining room were later additions.

In the Santa Fe rail days, when El Tovar needed to be reshingled, the railroad brought in a train of work and tool cars that housed the "B&B Gang," or Bridges and Buildings. When El Tovar needed repainting, a different train came in that housed the Paint Gang, and so on.

Major rehabilitation projects costing millions of dollars have kept the grande dame of the South Rim well preserved. A two-phase project in the mid-1970s brought the heating, cooling and electrical work up to date. In 1981, over $1.5 million was spent on rehabilitation of the exterior, which included insulation and replacement of windows with thermal pane and brown-tone aluminum frames. Fifty to sixty percent of the rotting exterior logs and wooden decking on balconies and porches was replaced.

After all of this work, Charles Whittlesey's turn-of-the-century creation still maintains the aristocratic atmosphere and Western intrigue it was intended to evoke as a destination for the elite.

Whittlesey's Alvarado Hotel was demolished in 1970 to make way for a parking lot, and the train

Always noted for its fine cuisine, El Tovar's tradition of elegant dining continues today.

station burned in January 1993. His Albuquerque home, a city landmark listed on the New Mexico State Register of Cultural Properties, is now the Albuquerque Press Club. In 1904, Whittlesey designed the Riordan Mansion in Flagstaff. The two-story, log-slab structure is two homes connected by a common room built for Tim and Mike Riordan and their families. With eighty rooms, eight bathrooms and seven fireplaces, it has many of the features of El Tovar, including the same kind of chandeliers that once hung in the its dining room. It is now the Riordan Mansion State Historic Park and on the National Register of Historic Places.

At the same time that Whittlesey was designing El Tovar, Mary Colter, a onetime Minnesota drawing and design teacher, was hired by Fred Harvey Company. Colter studied at the California School of Design and apprenticed in San Francisco. That California training influenced her career, the results best seen at the Grand Canyon. El Tovar was

Mary Colter's interest in indigenous peoples was key to her design of Hopi House built across from El Tovar. Hopi House opened just prior to El Tovar and displayed the Fred Harvey collection of prize-winning Navajo blankets.

the compound's flagship; Colter's design and decorating work fills the area. The Hopi House, directly across from El Tovar's entrance, exemplifies her rustic work. Other Colter buildings at the Grand Canyon include Bright Angel Lodge and Cabins, Hermit's Rest, the Lookout, the Watchtower (twenty miles from Grand Canyon Village) and Phantom Ranch, eight miles into the gorge.

The Santa Fe Railway and the Fred Harvey Company blazed a new trail in advertising and marketing of merchandise in conjunction with their train lines, stations and destination facilities. They introduced images of the Southwest and Indian arts, jewelry, rug and basketry to the rest of the country at world fairs and expositions, as well as in retail concerns. The Santa Fe hired and promoted artists and photographers (often using rail trips,

lodging and meals as payment) to capture the beauty of the Southwest. Under the direction of the company's general advertising agent, William Simpson, the railway acquired a vast art collection and became a corporate patron of the arts. Included was the 1907 Louis Akin painting "El Tovar Hotel, Grand Canyon." As early as 1902, the Indian Department of the Fred Harvey Company began collecting Native American art and artifacts to sell in its shops and to use for decorating. In 1978, the company donated the collection of more than 4,000 objects to the Heard Museum in Phoenix.

Fred Harvey, the family patriarch, died in 1901; his sons continued managing the South Rim facilities, purchasing them from the Santa Fe in 1954. The Fred Harvey Company became a subsidiary of Amfac, Inc., in 1968.

Today, the South Rim is congested with additional visitor facilities and the five million people who visit the Grand Canyon each year. Like the Indians who first discovered and explored the canyon over 10,000 years ago, many still gasp at their first sight of it. They peer down the one-mile-deep crevice and across the ten-mile span. The more adventuresome hike or take mules to the floor of the canyon to witness the geological story of ancient time.

El Tovar is a minor history lesson in itself, an architectural bridging of the era in which it was built. After the overpowering vistas of the Grand Canyon, guests can still find refuge in the comfort of the rambling hotel on the rim.

The redecorated Rendezvous Room is in keeping with the original rich decor.

Louis Hill, president of the Great Northern Railway, built his first Great Lodge at the edge of Glacier National Park.

Rail Baron's Dream Begins

Trains still run past Glacier Park Lodge as they did in 1913. Today, most visitors arrive by car or tour bus, but those who opt to take the train disembark at Glacier Park Station much like the first guests at the Lodge. Here, on what was the main transcontinental line of the Great Northern Railway, is Louis Hill's first Great Lodge.

Glacier National Park was established in 1910, thanks in part to the efforts of James J. Hill, founder of the Great Northern Railway, and his son, Louis. Louis Hill assumed the presidency of the railway in 1907, and while his father saw the park's potential as a draw for tourists—tourists who would arrive by train—it was Louis who had a burning passion for the project. He saw not only an opportunity to offer tourists an alternative to Yellowstone National Park, serviced by the Northern Pacific Railway, or the Grand Canyon, on a spur of the Atchison, Topeka & Santa Fe Railway line, but his chance to develop a project that was his own. His vision was a European system of roads and trails through the park with a series of back country chalets and major hotels to serve the guests.

The first superintendent of Glacier National Park and his Washington, D.C., colleagues were eager to accept the largess of the railway. Louis Hill was so dedicated to promoting Glacier National Park and the construction of his dream, that in December 1911, he temporarily stepped down as president of the Great Northern Railway to devote his time to these projects. "The work is so important that I am loath to intrust the development to anybody but myself," he explained to the press.

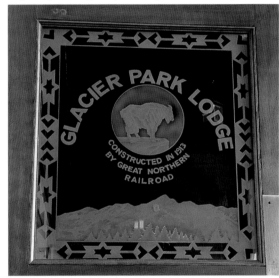

By 1912, Hill had secured a special Act of Congress giving the railroad the right to purchase 160 acres of land on the Blackfeet Indian Reservation just outside of the park at Midvale station (now Glacier Park Station). Here began the first of a building spree that would result in the construction of three major hotels (one in Waterton Lakes National Park, Glacier's adjoining "sister" park in Canada), nine chalets, miles of roads and trails—mostly in the eastern portion of the park—a telephone system and boat service.

Louis Hill combined his business resources, marketing savvy and political connections to pave the way for a construction project unequaled in any National Park. In addition, he masterminded a national advertising campaign combining the patriotic notion of "See America First" with the ironic coining of Glacier National Park as the "Alps of America." He entertained everyone from presidents to journalists in his relentless promoting of the park and his holdings. He hired artists, filmmakers and photographers to capture the beauty of the region, and took the exhibit on a special train to promote the park. European mountaineers were recruited to guide the tourists, and their ascents were heralded with ringing bells. His efforts paid off, and between 1910 and 1915 park visitation skyrocketed.

By the end of 1914, Glacier Park Hotel Company, a subsidiary of the Great Northern Railway, took over ownership and operation of the railway's hotels and camps in the park. What began as a short-term development project turned into a complex relationship between the Great Northern Railway and the U.S. government that would span over five decades. The combination of the Depression and the switch in travel tastes of the American public from rail car to automobile dramatically

LOCATION: East Glacier, Montana
OPENED: June 15, 1913
ARCHITECTS: S.L. Bartlett and Thomas D. McMahon
HISTORIC DESIGNATION: None

The great hall of Glacier Park Lodge, right, festooned with Japanese lanterns and hunting trophies, features the same huge, bark-covered log promenade as the Forestry Building, below. Louis Hill directed his architect to use the Forestry Building, constructed for Portland's 1905 Lewis and Clark Exposition, as the model for Glacier Park Lodge.

changed the park visitor dynamics; highway construction nearly doubled between 1927 and 1930. The railroad's tie to the park began to unravel.

As business decreased, a new animosity between the railway and the increasingly powerful National Park Service developed. Finally, in 1961, the Glacier Park Company (renamed during world War II while the hotels and chalets were closed for a period) sold its hotel and transportation interests in the park, East Glacier and Waterton Lakes National Park, Canada. But from 1911 through the 1920s, Louis Hill's vision was born and lived in all of its splendor.

What early train passengers found after their journey West across the great plains was a buffer between the huge yawn of the plains and the jagged teeth of the Rocky Mountains. Before encountering the "real" wilds of Glacier National Park, guests could decompress at a lodge big enough to be in keeping with its environment, yet as civilized as any Eastern or European hotel.

While Hill dubbed Glacier the "Alps of America," he wanted more than a chalet design for his first major hotel. Hill turned to the state of Oregon for inspiration. In 1905, the Oregon Historical Society sponsored the Lewis & Clark Exposition in Portland. Eleven states erected buildings, but the darling of the expo was the Oregon Forestry Building. Hill, and his father, James J. Hill, were particularly taken with the structure, which was meant to promote Oregon wood products. Other expositions had featured huge log buildings, but none quite as successfully as Portland architects Ion Lewis and then-apprentice Albert E. Doyle created with the Forestry Building. (Doyle later became one of Portland's premiere architects and submitted plans for a lodge on Mount Hood. Lewis was one of the architects who designed the original shingled

Cloud Cap Inn on Mount Hood.)

Massive forty-eight-foot-high logs formed the Forestry Building's colonnade. Skylights topped the pitched roof. In 1911, Hill had the plans, pictures and the cost of the structure sent to his architect, S.L. Bartlett. Hill's father had donated money to preserve and maintain the Forestry Building after the exposition, a donation that was noted in correspondence to acquire the plans. Bartlett had tracings made of the plans and returned them to Portland, as noted in a memo he wrote to Hill in September 1911. What Bartlett, with the assistance of Thomas McMahon, then created in Glacier Park Hotel (later changed to Lodge) was a chalet with a decidedly Western theme. Guests stepping off the train caught the panorama of the alpine Lodge set against the mountainous horizon. The manicured lawn was dotted with teepees, and the 1,000-foot garden path was banked with specially ordered flowers planted by the Swiss gardener. Blackfeet Indians served as hosts. After experiencing this collage of cultures, guests entered the front doors for their first forest experience. It was indoors.

The great hall is one of the most majestic of any of the Great Lodges of the West. The rectangular basilica design is derived from that of Roman halls, which was adopted as a building type for early Christian churches. Twenty-four forty-eight-foot-high, four-foot wide Douglas-firs line the colonnade of the 200- by 100-foot soaring lobby flanked by galleries on either side. Tree bark is intact on all of the vertical timbers (each weighing from fifteen to eighteen tons), giving the room the feel of a perfectly appointed forest. The eye immediately goes to the sky. Three atrium windows straddle the peak of the sixty-foot-high roof. Instead of green boughs, Ionic capitals top the mas-

Today, the Lodge's great hall is as grand as it was when guests first arrived.

Snow dusts the peaks of the Rocky Mountains as the seasons begin to change, and Glacier Park Lodge readies for its annual hibernation.

sive log columns. The space soars four stories, with peeled cedar railing along the two staggered balconies. St. Andrew's crosses are inset into the railing. The lobby is a sanctuary of sorts and reflects the idea of architecture as symbol, not just shelter. To Louis Hill, the symbol was based on European cathedrals, a place to praise both the beauty of the park and the free enterprise system that made the building possible.

When Hill's workers unloaded over sixty huge timbers, from thirty-six to forty inches in diameter and up to forty-eight feet long, from freight cars, the astounded Blackfeet are said to have dubbed the new building "Oom-Coo-Mush-Taw" or "Big Tree Lodge." It's no wonder. Trees of that size didn't grow in Montana, and since Hill wanted the same impressive colonnade as the Forestry Building, he had the firs sent by rail from the Pacific Northwest. By April 1912, all of the oversized timber for the hotel had been secured from "the coast." To ensure that the bark remain on the timbers, cutting had to take place before "sap running" in the spring. The Great Northern Railway had contracted with Evensta & Company of Minneapolis, to construct the building, and by March, Bartlett and the contractor were staking out the hotel, while a spur track was being completed to transport the timber now waiting at Whitefish and Essex. Construction began in April, and fifteen months later, the hotel was completed. The grand opening was held June 15, 1913, the 75th birthday of James J. Hill.

To say that Louis Hill was a "hands on" manager is an understatement. Hill not only negotiated concession agreements and land deals with the government, planned a parkwide concept of chalets and hotels linked by trails, a transportation system that included hiking, horses, cars, buses,

boats and trains, and kept his thumb on construction costs, but he personally selected everything for the decor, from paper lanterns to a mounted eagle his son had killed.

Hill's taste seemed as eclectic as his duties. Indian pictographs still decorate the walls above huge picture windows in the lobby. Animal horns and skins, buffalo skulls (some reproduced in plaster of Paris), teepees, Blackfeet crafts, rugs, blankets and basketry filled the lobby. To emphasize the "camp" feel of the "forest lobby," as a railway brochure of the time described it, was a copper-hooded, open fireplace at one end and a more traditional stone fireplace at the other. While totem poles stood on the front porch, Japanese lanterns hung from the rafters inside. The staff was part of the decor. Besides the Blackfeet Indians in their native garb, staff serving tea was dressed in kimonos, while others were outfitted in Bavarian uniforms. What the decor really reflected was the business interests of the Great Northern. The railway encouraged tourism to Seattle and Alaska, and its premiere train was called the Oriental Limited. The Great Northern also formed the Great Northern Steamship Co. to trade with Japan. If the decor with its advertising undercurrent was too confusing, guests could simply walk out on the expansive veranda running the length of the Lodge and gaze at the imposing mountain range artistically composed without the help of man.

Today, the lanterns and most of the original lobby furniture and accessories are gone. An original half-log table and baby grand piano remain, and a mountain goat (the Great Northern's mascot) is mounted in the center of the lobby. Three oversized chandeliers with Mission period lanterns and matching sconces light the space. Comfortable sofas and chairs fill the "reading" portion of the

main lobby. The hardwood floors remain, portions now carpeted. The open fireplace was removed after it caused more than a "camp" fire.

The cocktail lounge, once on the balcony, now fills half of the west lobby, with picture windows opening up the entire wall. At one time, the space served as the rest area for the Blackfeet, who besides working as hosts, put on evening shows for the guests. The small general store by the cocktail lounge was a coffee shop. The reception desk and gift shop now bank the east side of the lobby. Outside, oversized hickory chairs fill the veranda on the west, and flowers still line the garden path at the entry.

The dining room is not as imposing as some in other Great Lodges, but it offers a more, casual setting now decorated with red checked tablecloths, and Windsor-style chairs still surround the tables as they did in 1914. Wagon-wheel chandeliers that hang from the one-and-a-half-story ceiling have replaced at least two other vintages of light fixtures, including the original Japanese lanterns and the milk-glass globes of the 1940s. The original clinker brick fireplace, with hooks and a simmering shelf, anchors one wall, and eighteen-inch log columns support the structure.

The basement featured a cabaret area with a bar. What is now the Feather Room cabaret used for evening shows was once the plunge swimming pool.

Almost as soon as the sixty-one-room hotel was completed, Hill ordered an addition. A four-story annex, connected by a wide breezeway, added 111 rooms to the hotel. The breezeway created one of the most charming additions to the Lodge, a definite departure from the huge, imposing great hall. The breezeway is banked on both sides by windows and topped with the timber beams and

trusses of the open ceiling. Filled with Morris chairs, card tables and desks, it is used today as it was originally intended. Guests read, write letters, play cards or enjoy the scenery from a sunny, sheltered vantage point. By the time the annex was completed, the Glacier Park Lodge cost $500,000 to construct and furnish.

Guest rooms were intended for the sophisticated traveler. Private baths, fireplaces, porches and suites were all available. Each room was meticulously furnished, and some of the guest-room pieces remain in the Lodge. Glass shades were custom-ordered from Pittsburgh and rooms were decorated with sturdy oak furniture, Navajo rugs, china candlesticks and Hudson Bay blankets.

The exterior of both the main Lodge and annex features a pitched roofline with long shed dormers running nearly the entire length of the roof. Arched brace roofs extend over balconies in the annex (in much the same fashion as the Forestry Building), supported by massive timbers, with jigsawn balustrades between board railings that add a Swiss touch. The main building has peeled log railings along the balconies and porches and shingles between the gables. The plan originally called for log exterior on the main building, but was changed to clapboard siding and shingles. The wood is painted "National Park" brown. The Great Northern hotels were originally coated with a creosote stain.

Besides the natural beauty, Glacier Park Lodge has a golf course, built in

1928, and an outdoor swimming pool. The railroad sold its hotels in 1960 to Donald Hummel, who formed Glacier Park, Inc. In 1981, Hummel sold his Glacier holdings to The Dial Corp. Today, Glacier Park Lodge is owned and operated by Glacier Park, Inc., now a subsidiary of Viad Corp. Amazingly, the Lodge has not been nominated for historic landmark designation.

It takes little imagination to transport oneself back to 1913 here on the edge of Glacier National Park. As a train whistle blows or a party of riders pass by on horseback, guests can still quietly rock in one of the huge hickory chairs, and watch the sun fade behind the Rockies.

Members of the Blackfeet tribe were among the greeters welcoming guests as they arrived in "buses" at Glacier Park Lodge.

Red "Jammers" relay tourists from Lake McDonald Lodge to other lodges and points of interest in Glacier National Park.

Exquisite in Every Detail

Glacier National Park is sliced by the Continental Divide. On the east side of the wall of rock, Louis Hill and the Great Northern Railway dominated development. Hill demanded control, and while the railway built a chalet for passengers at the Belton station, major development was on the east side. The Rocky Mountains gave him a natural barrier from the "riff raff" that ran hunting lodges and the budding bureaucracy of the National Park Service that eventually built its headquarters in what is now West Glacier.

In the 1890s, homesteaders settled on the shores of Lake McDonald, where they trapped game and considered other means of survival. In 1895, George Snyder built the Snyder Hotel on the present site of Lake McDonald Lodge. Between 1904 and 1905, John Lewis, a businessman and fur trader from Columbia Falls, Montana, gained control of the Snyder Hotel and the 285 acres surrounding it. Lewis had maintained a fishing and tourist camp at Lake McDonald, and with Glacier designated a National Park in 1910, he saw a niche for his own upgraded operation. Lewis admired the alpine chalet design of Hill's Belton Chalet and the grand Glacier Park Hotel, and if he couldn't fund something as large, at least he would equal its

style. Lewis commissioned Kirtland Cutter of Spokane, Washington, to design the Lodge.

Cutter was trained in New York and Europe as an artist, not a draftsman. In 1886, he moved from his home in Cleveland, Ohio to Spokane, where the riches of mining were making the fledgling city a mecca for banking and building. Cutter's uncle

worked for a Spokane bank, and Cutter's first job was there. The charming and gifted artist soon found his way into architecture. By the time he met Lewis, he had established a reputation for creating mansions for the Spokane elite. What set Cutter apart from the crowd, all vying to design a home more spectacular than the last, was his interest in merging the local material, most notably volcanic rock and cedar, with his plans. His early work reflected the expanded English cottage style and

Arts and Crafts Movement of the era. Cutter also admired the work of Swiss architects, and this influence is seen at Lake McDonald Lodge.

Cutter's first significant experiments with Swiss chalet design were the Idaho Building he designed with his partner John Poetz for the 1893 World's Columbian Exposition in Chicago, and his own home on South Hill in Spokane. The Idaho Building commission, meant to reflect the style and substance of the state, featured charming Swiss detailing countered by the use of huge timbers and a first floor of rough basalt rock. The three-story log building had a low, sloping roof topped with rocks in the Swiss tradition. The wide eaves were supported by corbeled log brackets, and a huge stone entry anchored one end. Balconies featured log railing with St. Andrew's cross balustrades. The Idaho Building had many of the same features as his home, begun in 1888, and the hotel on the shores of Lake McDonald.

Lewis relocated the old Snyder Hotel to make way for the new hotel. When Cutter designed the Lewis Glacier Hotel (now Lake McDonald Lodge), access to the site was from the lake. Guests arrived by train at the Belton station and were ferried by

LOCATION: Glacier National Park, Montana
OPENED: June 1914 (as the Lewis Glacier Hotel)
ARCHITECT: Kirtland Cutter
HISTORIC DESIGNATION: National Historic Landmark, May 28, 1987

steam boat to the Lodge. So, the first impression included an incredible entrance—the often glassy span of the beautiful lake. What they saw as they cruised across the lake was a perfect alpine chalet nestled in the woods. It was on this very route that materials to build Lake McDonald Lodge were transported. With no roads or rail access, building supplies were brought to the site by boat until the lake froze in the winter. Then supplies were skidded across the ice. Concrete and foundation work was completed before the winter of 1913. The sixty-five-room hotel opened in June 1914 at a cost of $48,000.

The main portion of the three-and-one-half-story structure is built on a concrete foundation. The exterior finish is a combination of white stucco and wood clapboarding painted the same brown as the Great Northern's hotels. Multiple balconies and jigsawn decorative bands of wood separate and define the floors. The same jigsawn detail frames windows and doors. Log columns support the first balcony with log railings and balustrades. On the lake side of the building, the bark remains on the post-and-beam balcony support. The gabled roof was originally topped, again in the traditional Swiss manner, with logs and stones that were removed

sometime between 1920 and 1930. Deep eaves are supported by squared timbers with profiled ends.

Swiss alpine design dominates the exterior, but inside John Lewis and Kirtland Cutter created the "Wild West." Concrete floors are scored to look like flagstone, with incised phrases in Blackfeet, Chippewa and Cree ("welcome," "new life to those who drink here," "looking toward the mountain," and "big feast"). The three-story lobby has a decorative log-trussed ceiling and is banked by balconies on three sides featuring bark-covered cedar log railings and balustrades. Cutter, who was not fond of the skylights at Glacier Park Lodge, let the

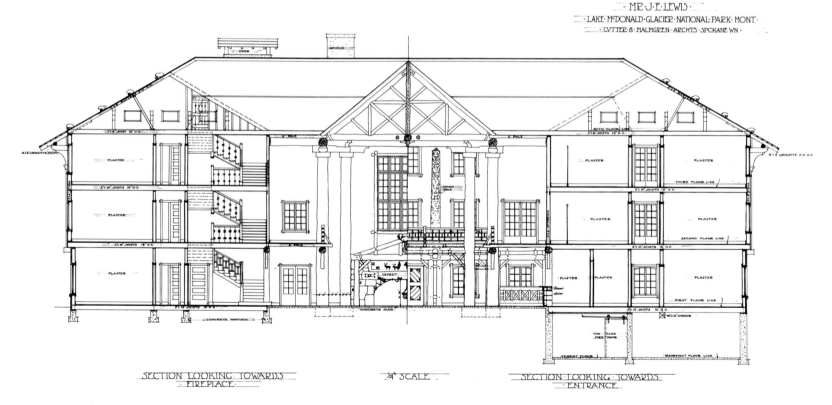

Kirtland Cutter designed the Lewis Glacier Hotel (later named Lake McDonald Lodge). His cross-section drawing shows the two-story, mullioned, multi-pane windows above the fireplace.

In 1920, guests still arrived by boat to the Swiss chalet-design hotel on Lake McDonald.

Below: Inside, the Swiss chalet was transformed into a Montana hunting lodge.

sun shine in through a two-story paned window above the fireplace. The huge hearth is framed by Indian designs scored and painted around the opening. Montana artist Charles Russell, a friend of Lewis and his wife, was a frequent visitor to the Lodge. Speculation is that Russell created the fireplace designs. The lobby corners feature columns each made from three large Western-cedar logs that support the log floor structure of the balconies. Bark remains on the columns and much of the other log work. Two stairways made with burled wood newel posts and jigsawn balustrades offer a whimsical contrast to the rustic interior.

Lewis was an avid traveler, collector and hunter; elk, antelope, moose, goat, eagle and mountain sheep hunting trophies hung on the columns and walls, and animal skins and Navajo rugs were draped from the balconies. Frank Stick and H. Bartlett oil paintings and Fred Kiser photographs filled the walls, and artists, tourists and trappers alike swapped stories in the perfectly designed and appointed lobby.

Guest rooms were off both sides of the lobby and on the upper floors. A separate wing to the south of the lobby housed the dining room and kitchen, offering everything tourists required: a place to eat, sleep and a perfect hunting lodge "salon" in which to socialize.

While the arrival to the remote Lodge by boat was charming, Lewis understood the changing times and lobbied for a road. The Great Northern was building roads in East Glacier, but politics bogged down the West-side road development. In 1919, Lewis built three and a half miles of road on the eastern side of Lake McDonald with his own funds. Lewis' initial $3,200 investment provided an important link to what would become the $3 million Going to the Sun Highway, which was completed in July 1933.

In 1920, road work continued under park jurisdiction, and by the late summer of 1921, rough road access to the Lodge was completed, and guests began arriving through the "back door." A balcony was added and the back was spruced up as the new entrance. Now, with guests entering from both sides of the building, the original design began to lose its integrity. A bank of guest rooms was added in 1934 on the second and third floors along the lake side, changing both the interior and exterior. The following year, a large parking area was added as part of the road improvements of the time. But the "new" entrance was neither elegant nor impressive. During parking lot construction, regrading left a seven-foot berm of dirt at the new entrance, giving guests walking from the parking lot a view straight into the second-floor rooms.

Progress was not helping the hotel. John Lewis sold the hotel to the National Park Service in 1930 in a complicated financial deal that included the Great Northern Railway. Glacier Park Hotel Co., a subsidiary of the railway, became the concessionaire and changed the name to Lake McDonald Hotel. In 1960, the Lodge came under the management of Donald Hummel; he sold his Glacier interests to The Dial Corp in 1981.

Over the years, a flood, reconfiguration and remodeling bore down on the original structure and eroded the character of the Lodge. As times changed, a gift shop, offices, suitcase storage and a registration desk encroached on the impressive lobby. Sitting in the midst of the once idyllic lobby was no longer a pleasant experience. That changed in 1988-89 when Lake McDonald Lodge underwent a $1.2 million rehabilitation.

One of the goals of the project was to restore the flavor and details used in the 1914 construction and bring back the ambiance that had been lost

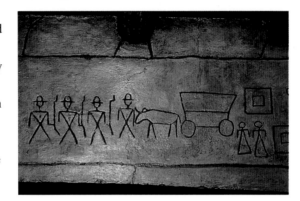

Pictographs incised above the hearth.

over time. "It surpasses the other lodges at Glacier," explained Paul Newman, renovation project manager and historical architect for the National Park Service. "Lake McDonald Lodge may not be as grand as the other Glacier Park hotels, but the detail is spectacular."

In the lobby, damaged cedar logs or bark were replaced and the infrastructure upgraded. The registration desk was sunk into the edge of the lobby in what used to be a guest room, and the original circulation pattern was restored by moving other services that cluttered the space. An historical paint analysis revealed the original terra-cotta paint and stencil pattern, which was restored. The fabulous fireplace and inglenook were cleaned and

renovated. A remodeled gift shop, cocktail lounge, relocated restrooms and accessible guest rooms were incorporated into the plan. All of these additions got new plumbing and electrical systems.

Unlike the other Glacier Park lodges, many of the original hunting trophies and pieces of furniture remained in the Lodge. Some of the hickory chairs, notably those with thick log legs and arms or cane seats are of historic significance. The large oak table with cedar-bark-covered base in the lobby is original. The huge slab table in the south corner of the lobby is original, as are the upright piano and scalloped-back chairs. Reproductions, including many hickory pieces from the Old Hickory Furniture Co., of Indiana, were ordered and lobby rugs were designed and woven to match the color and pattern of original Gustav Stickley area rugs. A group of Roycroft crafters produced three couches to look like the originals.

The distinctive shades hanging in the lobby and dining room were originally painted by the Blood Indians and hung in the Prince of Wales Hotel in Waterton Lakes National Park, Canada. In the 1960s, they were moved to Lake McDonald, and in 1982, Montana artist Kay Storms was commissioned to reproduce the deteriorating shades using the original framework.

Besides bringing back the rustic feel of the decor and much of the integrity of Cutter's design, the renovation uncovered some of the Lodge's history.

The dining room—nearly wiped out in the flood of 1964 that tore through Snyder Creek—was one such story. Architectural drawings for the dining wing were never found, only Cutter's connection plans to the room. According to Paul Newman, the dining room was constructed from an assemblage of on-site buildings. A larger log build-

Two open stairways off the lobby feature burled newel posts and sapling jigsawn balustrades. Wall colors and border design, part of the renovation, are circa 1923.

furniture (about sixty percent of the furniture is original). At night, the room glows from the light of hand-painted shades and Arts and Crafts period sconces. Daylight shines through windows in keeping with the original design that replaced the plate glass, post-flood versions. The twofold goal to bring the room back to its original intent and successfully deal with accessibility was met.

On the exterior, cracked stucco on crumbling brick and rotted wood was replaced. The roadside entrance was made more inviting by eliminating the dirt berm, gently terracing the grade and taking out the steep stairs. One of the finishing touches was to restore a Lodge icon. Lewis had acquired a totem pole on his travels to southeastern Alaska, and while the pole was long gone, photographs of it were analyzed and a replica commissioned from an Alaskan carver.

On the lake side of the Lodge, in addition to the original porch lined with hickory rockers, lovely new terraces and seating areas, and walkways to the boat docks now unify the lake and Lodge. Native stone was used for the walls, and the same technique of scored concrete originally used in the lobby was repeated outdoors. The grounds are landscaped with native plants; annuals fill the baskets and planters as they did in 1914.

Renovation began on October 14, 1988, but it was not to be an easy project. Weather was typical—snow depths of two feet and temperatures from ninety degrees to minus thirty degrees. It wasn't the Arctic wind or snow that stopped construction, but the American bald eagle. Prior to construction work, the National Park Service naturalists had advised the crew that construction could not disturb the migratory or nesting eagles.

ing is the center of the structure with two log cabins hooked together to create additional dining space and the kitchen wing. During the renovation, work revealed a foundation that was not the same quality as the rest of the building. However the room was assembled, when complete, the original dining room created a strong axis terminating at the fireplace. The flood had destroyed the fireplace and the integrity of the room.

Now guests are drawn into a warm and inviting room, as they enter an intimate upper level dining space, then follow steps into the main room. The fireplace, again the focal point at the far end of the room, was rebuilt from local river stone. The walls, replaced after the flood with studs and plywood, were restored with squared cedar logs, each one individually hand-worked to replicate the originals. Hardwood floors complement the wood

Hence, the contract called for fifty-four days whereby construction could cease, and fifty-six were specified for only night work. From November 20 to December 31, 1988, no work of any type was allowed at the site, and from March 18 through April 23, 1989, only night work was allowed. The Lodge opened for operation that season, and detail work was completed over the summer.

The National Park Service owns fee title to the building and some of the furnishings, and Glacier Park, Inc., a subsidiary of Viad Corp, (formerly The Dial Corp) has compensable interest in the rest of the lodge's furnishings. GPI manages the Lake McDonald complex under a contract with the NPS.

Besides the Lodge, the Lake McDonald Historic District includes a cluster of cabins built between 1907 and 1908. These have been updated over time and are rented to guests. The entire complex has a camp village atmosphere with dorms, first-aid station, general store and an auditorium/chapel. A family-style restaurant, built during the NPS Mission 66 phase, is functional but out of character with the area and is an example of what might have happened to the architecture of the district if expansion plans had been completed at that time.

One need look no further than the small rise where the Lake McDonald Lodge stands for alpine architectural inspiration. The merging of the Swiss chalet with Montana hunting lodge is delightfully played out in this gem on the shores of Glacier's largest lake.

Decorative brackets supporting eaves and white jigsawn trim are all Swiss chalet details Kirtland Cutter delighted in using.

Guests arriving at Many Glacier Hotel.

Magnificent Yet Endangered Historic Structure

If hotel guests got their first glimpse of Glacier National Park from Glacier Park Lodge, it was fifty-three miles away at the end of a twelve-mile road through the Swiftcurrent Valley where they experienced the full impact of the park. Many Glacier Hotel, the second hotel built by Louis Hill and the Great Northern Railway, follows the contours of Swiftcurrent Lake. Beyond the lake and fir, spruce and lodgepole pine forest are two more lakes and the massive glaciated peaks of Grinnell Point, Mount Wilbur, Mount Henkel and Mount Gould. Two walls of jagged rock, Pfarmigan and Garden, and three glaciers create what seems like an impenetrable barrier. Here is a pocket of glacial carving and erosion that is overpowering in its beauty. It is a place where one is seemingly locked in by the geography. Out "there" in the wilds were the bear, deer, beavers and fowl. Inside, the animals were stuffed, and the beauty man-made. While larger than its counterpart in East Glacier, Many Glacier Hotel, built like a series of chalets, is set in the midst of such natural grandeur, it seems slightly less daunting.

Louis Hill picked the site for the second hotel in 1909. As with many of his developments, Hill provided much of the crew and Evensta & Company of Minneapolis was again selected as the contractor. Thomas McMahon, who was one of the architects for Glacier Park Lodge, designed a four-

and-one-half story hotel in three separate structures. The main lobby and guest rooms that now make up the center of the complex were built in five months; an annex to the north with the dining room and kitchen was then built. In 1917, a second annex was constructed to the south with sixty-seven guest rooms, and was connected by an expansive breezeway topped with a decorative cupola. In the 1950s a porte-cochère was added at the entrance, topped with a spire meant to complement the one on the breezeway.

Hill and Ralph Budd, acting president of the Great Northern while Hill devoted his time to the Glacier projects, both courted noted Spokane architect Kirtland Cutter to provide plans for the site. John Lewis had hired Cutter to design the exquisite Lake McDonald Lodge (then called the Lewis Glacier Hotel) that opened in June 1914. Hill, Cutter and Thomas McMahon visited the park in the spring of 1914, and both architects proceeded with preliminary plans. Cutter submitted at least two sets of pencil-sketch plans and blueprints. But Hill wasn't satisfied, and by July, Hill noted in correspondence, "We have not the plans perfected yet and will not do any thing on this building this year…" By early fall, Hill decided to use McMahon as the architect. A disappointed Cutter billed the Great Northern Railway $1,000 "for services rendered." Hill reluctantly paid, and McMahon proceeded.

LOCATION: Glacier National Park, Montana
OPENED: July 4, 1915 (Annex completed in 1917)
ARCHITECT: Thomas D. McMahon
HISTORIC DESIGNATION: National Historic Landmark, May 28, 1987

In 1940, Many Glacier Hotel's great hall still had the circular stairway and rock fountain.

The design of Many Glacier Hotel is a blend of the Bartlett/McMahon Glacier Park Lodge (based on the Forestry Building of the 1905 Lewis & Clark Exposition in Portland) and Cutter's original drawings. If Louis Hill felt, "…we had not derived much benefit from Cutter's work," to the nonprofessional eye, Cutter's exterior sketches for the Many Glaciers Camp hotel, now at the Washington State Historical Society in Spokane, could have been the basis for the Hotel that now stands. And surely, it was.

The Swiss chalet architecture combined with timbers and native rock—a hallmark of Cutter's Lake McDonald Lodge, the Idaho Building for which he won a gold medal at the 1893 World's Columbian Exposition in Chicago, and his own home in Spokane—is prevalent at Many Glacier. Cutter's Many Glaciers elevation drawing from the lake side shows the lobby turned to face the lake, first-floor stonework with arched windows, tiered balconies and a gabled roof topped with a cupola. With the exception of the cupola, McMahon incorporated these designs in his plans. Eventually two cupolas were built atop two later additions—the breezeway and porte-cochère. The other elements are part of Many Glacier Hotel. Cutter proposed a lobby with columns, each one made of four twelve-inch trees (much the same design as the Idaho Building and Lake McDonald Lodge) with upper windows on both sides and under the gables, instead of the skylights used at Glacier Park Lodge.

Even with its Swiss chalet architecture, Many Glacier Hotel is primarily built of material native to the area. While the great hall is basically the same as Glacier Park Lodge, Many Glacier's lobby is half the size. The skylights that Cutter discarded were repeated here. And once again, the massive single support timbers were brought from Washington

and Oregon by the Great Northern, then skidded by horse to the building site. The other timber used is spruce, locally harvested from the Grinnell Lake area, then carried by floats across Lake Josephine and Swiftcurrent Lake. Hill negotiated timber harvesting and sales from 1910 through 1914. A sawmill was set up for the project on site, where Hill also built a planing mill and kiln. (A decade later, Stephen Mather, director of the National Park Service, would have the mill dynamited in a show of pique and power after Hill refused to follow his orders to have it demolished.)

While Hill waited for timber permits, excavation, stone and preparatory work was taking place at the site; there was hardly a lull in development. By the time the Many Glacier Hotel construction began, eight of the nine chalets in his grand plan had been completed.

The Hotel was the main structure in a group of proposed buildings for the site. By December, framing was up for the dormitory, and stone foundation for the main Hotel had been laid. Stone for the foundation, the waterfront terrace, with its segmental arched windows and doors, was quarried from the area. McMahon was pleased. "The stone in this foundation comes practically square...it was laid as it came from the mountain," he relayed to Hill in December 1914 correspondence that was accompanied by photos. By January, bridge builders from the Great Northern put the forty-foot timbers in place for the lobby, and the dormitory wing, bridge and dining room were under construction.

The huge timbers in Many Glacier Hotel are without bark. Whether the logs were peeled because the bark was damaged in transit or logged too late in the season is unknown. Instead of the rustic log balustrades and railings of Glacier Park

Lodge, hand-carved balustrades bring the chalet look of the Many Glacier exterior inside. Three balconies line two sides of the lobby with guest rooms off them; the third floor (crow's nest) is used as employee housing. A stairway is at each end of the lobby. Board and batten wainscoting with white fiberboard above and St. Andrew's crosses on the guest-room doors add to the Swiss theme.

When Many Glacier opened it had the feeling of a hybrid hunting lodge. The heavy Swiss motif —down to the red and white crosses on every guest-room door or the Japanese lanterns hanging from the wooden rafters and umbrellas secured in logs on the orange floor of the great hall—didn't overshadow the Western theme. Buffalo skulls, some made of plaster of Paris, and over a dozen silvertip (grizzly) bear skins hung from the balco-

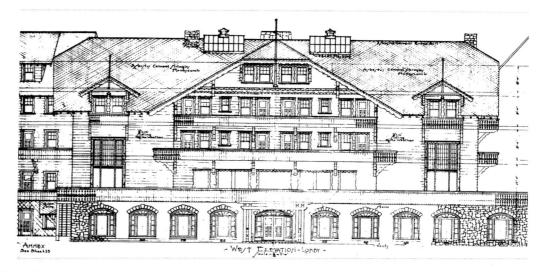

Thomas D. McMahon's elevation drawing, above, shows many of the same elements as Kirtland Cutter's preliminary pencil/tissue drawings, below. Louis Hill did not retain Cutter, rather turned over the design work for Many Glacier Hotel to McMahon.

Canoes stand ready for tourists to glide them across Swiftcurrent Lake.

Segmental arched windows are built from locally quarried stone.

nies. A moose head above the gift shop is all that remains of the lobby's original hunting trophies. (The ram in the lobby was the victim of a fall through the skylight one winter.) A 180-foot mural, painted in panels by Blackfeet artists, covered an entire wall. Totem poles (seven were ordered from the Pacific Northwest) dotted the lobby.

Rather than fill the space with sofas and lounge chairs, Hill chose a variety of seemingly "disposable" furniture: dozens of Japanese wicker, Windsor and canvas-folding chairs cluttered the room. As spring of 1915 approached, Hill was busy ordering everything from checker and chess sets to bundles of bamboo fishing poles for decorating the Grill Room.

A miniature mountain of sorts was created at the south end of the great hall. A spiral stairway that led to the Bamboo Room (now the St. Moritz Room) wound around a fountain built from native rock and decorated with ferns. Colored lights shone on the fountain and trout swam in the pond at its base. The same hand-carved balustrades featured on the balconies surrounded the stairway opening. Music from dance bands downstairs rose into the lobby, one of the reasons given for its removal in 1957. More likely it was to expand the

gift shop that was extended twenty feet into the lobby. This protruding gift shop, even with a stuffed ram sitting atop the front wall, detracts from the overall impact of the room. A firepit still stands at the north end of the lobby with a huge copper hood suspended over the native stone base, where a fire burns each day and night. A rustic stone fireplace is near the entrance, along with over twenty others in the Hotel, all nonfunctioning today.

The single-story dining room at Many Glacier is not off the great hall as is the usual lodge floor plan. Instead, diners meander down a corridor of guest rooms, through a breezeway (now the Interlaken Lounge) to the Ptarmigan Dining Room.

Today, Swiss banners hang from the ceiling. Anchored by a huge stone fireplace, the room is blessed with floor-to-ceiling windows along the west wall and on each side of the fireplace. Original paintings commissioned by Hill and created by German artist J. Fery hang at the dining room entrance.

As with Glacier Park Lodge, the new Hotel did not meet the demand for rooms. An eighty-room annex was completed in 1917, and as construction prices climbed, Hill demanded an accounting report that compared the recently completed Paradise Inn at Mount Rainier, Washington (Hill thought it had been built for $40,000) to the Many Glacier Hotel. "They seem to have some economical way of

Views seen from the Many Glacier Hotel veranda are spectacular.

Horses line up at the hitchrack in front of the hotel in 1931, prior to the cupola-topped porte-cochère addition. Opposite: Swiss banners add an international touch to Many Glacier Hotel dining room.

The original Indian-carved bear lamps are gone, and the handmade tables and chairs were discarded by past concessionaires. Baths were remodeled and added in the 1950s. This remodeling was part of a $1.5 million renovation carried out by the Great Northern in hopes of sprucing up the hotels to sell them. Many Glacier was the main target for "renovation." Linoleum tile floors replaced the original hardwood (now carpeted), the spiral stairway was removed, several guest rooms were removed next to the breezeway, and the Swiss Lounge was constructed. Much of the work detracted from the historic integrity of the building, but the Swiss Lounge reflects the same detail the railroad was known for. Outside of the lounge are two Charles de Feo oil paintings.

Many Glacier's basement showcases the detailed stonework that so pleased McMahon. The stone basement walls and foundations, with the beautifully arched windows along the lake side walls are set on two- to three-foot-wide stone pads. In Many Glacier's heyday, an indoor swimming pool filled part of the basement level. Two "theater" spaces remain: the Lucerne Room suffered from renovation (encasing of the original beams and painting it an institutional gray), while the St. Moritz Room retains much of its charm. The original Grill Room and bar is gone, and the space is now a small general store. Lake access rooms (originally "value rooms") are now used for bellmen and maintenance personnel. A walk down the basement hallway—referred to as the stagger alley—reveals the skewing of the structure that takes place each winter when twenty-foot drifts of snow crush in on the building.

Besides the annual snow fall, Many Glacier Hotel has survived catastrophic fires and floods. On August 31, 1936, one of Montana's forest fires

doing this work," Hill noted in an October 16 memo to Ralph Budd. McMahon complied and provided a comparative study. It was obvious the Great Northern was building a much larger, far more luxurious and sophisticated structure, and one much farther from any metropolitan area than the Paradise Inn. When completed, the Many Glacier Hotel featured steam heat, electric lights, hot and cold water, an indoor plunge pool and over twenty fireplaces at a total cost of $500,000.

The exterior is "National Park brown" with yellow jigsawn trim and white window frames. The roofline is a variety of gables, many finished with clipped-gable ends. Long dormers and hip roofs are finished with wood shingles.

Guest rooms, particularly those on the lake side with balconies, are old but charming. There is no more spectacular way to start a day than to step out of your room and see the mirror reflection of the mountains in the calm of Swiftcurrent Lake.

suddenly broke through fire lines and raced towards the Swiftcurrent Valley and Many Glacier Hotel. Guests were evacuated by bus. The fire engulfed four chalets as it moved towards Swiftcurrent Lake. Burning forest debris flew across the lake and hit the Hotel, but the main blaze blew around the Hotel. Staff fought the flames and saved the structure, then in jubilation of their feat, wired the Great Northern headquarters: "WE HAVE SAVED THE HOTEL!" By then the hotels were losing propositions for the railway; the terse telegram reply read: "WHY?"

In 1960, long after their usefulness to the Great Northern, the hotels were sold to Donald Hummel of Arizona. Hummel formed Glacier Park, Inc., and ran the hotels for twenty years, selling the operation to The Dial Corp in 1981. During that time, Hummel and Many Glacier Hotel manager Ian Tippet instituted the musical programs performed by staff that remain the highlight for many guests.

Today, the National Park Service owns fee title to the Many Glacier Hotel complex. Glacier Park, Inc., a subsidiary of Viad Corp (formerly The Dial Corp) has a compensable interest in the facilities and owns its furnishings. Hundreds of thousands of dollars have been spent over the years on maintenance and upkeep, and GPI in conjunction with the NPS, hopes to continue the effort. It is a huge task. The Many Glacier Hotel is one of the Great Lodges of the West, but in 1996, it, along with other Glacier Park buildings, was included in the National

Trust for Historic Preservation's list of "America's 11 Most Endangered Historic Places." In 1996, an estimate for its *basic* rehabilitation was $30 million.

Still, eight decades after Many Glacier Hotel was built, Hill's genius in melding the wilds of Montana with what is now a historic landmark remains. The best way to understand the relationship of Many Glacier Hotel to Glacier National Park is by boat. As *Chief Two Guns,* one of the original wooden crafts, chugs across Swiftcurrent Lake on its early morning excursion, you'll find yourself caught between two worlds: to the east is a fabulous building and to the west the mountains that can only humble it.

The once decrepit Crater Lake Lodge was born again through a $15 million rehabilitation.

The Building Oregonians Wouldn't Let Die

At the end of May 1995, fifteen to twenty feet of snow still covered the landscape at Oregon's Crater Lake in the southern portion of the Cascade Range. But it wasn't the spectacle of one of the wonders of the world caught between seasons that drew the crowds. Nor was it the blue waters that fill the deepest lake in America, created almost 8,000 years ago when Mount Mazama's final eruption blew ash over eight states and three Canadian provinces. They were there to see the building that the people of Oregon wouldn't let die.

Crater Lake Lodge reopened on May 20, 1995, after six years and $15 million of painstaking renovation. Visitors filled the seventy-one perfectly appointed rooms in hopes of recapturing memories of honeymoons and family vacations. These same memories created such a flood of protest that when the National Park Service recommended its demolition, engineers and contractors ended up dismantling the structure and putting it back together. This time, the engineers, contractors and designers built a Lodge that could hold not only memories, but also the tons of snow that pile on the rooftop and the thirty-foot drifts that bank the walls.

The truth is that the old Lodge, built in bursts beginning in 1909, was a dump. The roof sagged, the bathrooms were Spartan, light fixtures dangled from the ceiling, and the wind whipped through the walls. From a distance, it had the stature of a Great Lodge. But up close, it was a hodgepodge of neglect—an elegant idea that was never completed, but periodically patched up. After decades of debate, various concessionaires, volumes of governmental structural and safety reports, and changing National Park Service priorities, the Lodge was closed in 1989.

The construction and deterioration of Crater Lake Lodge and the public and political haggling that swirled around it are part of its history. It took fifty years from the time the first white explorers tramped in the Cascade Range for a prospector to find Crater Lake. In 1853, while searching for gold, John Wesley Hillman stumbled upon the huge caldera. Laid out before him was not the glitter of gold but what is now called the bluest lake in the world. With a depth of almost 2,000 feet and a skirt of pumice, Crater Lake is one of nature's majestic surprises.

William G. Steel, an Ohio native, hiked to the rim of Crater Lake in 1885; he was awestruck by the scene. He returned in 1896 as part of the Mazama mountaineering club to promote the lake and its surroundings as a candidate for a National Park. In 1902, Crater Lake National Park was established, mostly through the seventeen-year crusade by Steel, and with it came the real possibility of building a hotel. Steel spearheaded the Crater Lake Improvement Association, and in 1907, he formed the Crater Lake Company. As its president, one of his first projects was Camp Crater, a modest tent city where tourists spent the night. Visitors got primitive lodging, hot meals and the chance to indulge in the spectacular surroundings. Steel longed for grander things—steamboats cruising to Wizard Island, elevators descending to the water's edge and two hotels. Steel knew he could not do this alone.

Initially, Steel hoped for financial backing from the Southern Pacific Railway. The kind of funding and the rail lines that made Old Faithful Inn, El Tovar Hotel and the lodges of Glacier National Park possible never materialized. In 1909, Steel named Portland developer and real estate associate Alfred L. Parkhurst as the company's general manager and major stockholder. Parkhurst's first project was

LOCATION: Crater Lake National Park, Oregon
OPENED: June 28, 1915; (Reopened) May 20, 1995
ARCHITECT: (Original) Raymond Hockenberry; (Rehabilitation) Fletcher Farr Ayotte, Portland
HISTORIC DESIGNATION: National Register of Historic Places, 1981

*Heavy snow blankets
Crater Lake Lodge, 1927.*

the stone-and-wood Lodge on the edge of the caldera. Parkhurst hired contractor Frank Keyes to take on the daunting task of constructing the Lodge during the few months the area wasn't buried in snow. R.H. Hockenberry & Co. was commissioned to draw architectural plans. Hockenberry was the architect for several Portland residences that are now on the National Register.

When Crater Lake Lodge construction began, few lodges existed at high elevations with heavy snow conditions. Parkhurst and Hockenberry could have turned to Cloud Cap Inn on Mount Hood, also in the Cascade Range, or a smaller version of Robert Reamer's Old Faithful Inn at Yellowstone. Instead, Hockenberry followed Parkhurst's lead and his own experience, and designed a lodge that combined the idea of an "auto-lodge" with a suburban house, relying on a mock Tudor design. While later lodges like those

The Lodge appears to hug the rim of America's deepest lake in this early (undated) photograph.

in Glacier National Park, Mount Rainier National Park and Mt. Hood National Forest were constructed of heavy timbers and logs, Crater Lake Lodge was basically a light wood-frame building much like homes of the period.

Originally conceived as an all wood structure, plans were changed, and the first floor incorporated native rock in its masonry walls. Three rectangular sections ran along the edge of the caldera with a kitchen wing joined on the south end at a ninety-degree angle. Three stone chimneys were part of the exterior for fireplaces in the dining hall, great hall and west wall of the lobby (intended for gatherings, but used only once because of chimney fires). Guest rooms were above.

While the roof was steeply pitched, each ridge came to a jerkinhead gable rather than a traditional gable. Eaves begin just above the second story with shed roof dormers for the third-story rooms

Striped tents added a festive air as early Lodge construction began.

Mark Daniels' 1914 vision of the great hall, with European stenciling and additional supports, was never executed.

and a row of fourth-story dormers. The lobby or great hall roof was slightly higher, and the kitchen wing only two stories, giving variety to the roofline. The roof, according to a newspaper interview with Keyes, was to be tiling, and "...will defy the ravages of the elements for all time to come." Instead, it was shingled with wood and eventually stained a dark green.

Building the Lodge was a task few at the time would consider and one Parkhurst and Keyes underestimated. The project was never properly funded. From the original estimate of $5,000, the cost soon soared to $30,000. Keyes often ignored Hockenberry's plans, taking shortcuts to save money. The contractor struggled to get the necessary equipment and supplies for the project. Timber, rocks and stone were in abundant supply, but quarrying the stone and moving the timber to the site were fraught with mishaps. Getting supplies to the edge of Crater Lake was just a fraction of the battle. In 1911, Parkhurst reported that lumber was at the construction site, but he couldn't secure carpenters to do the work. As the Lodge slowly took form each summer, winter would ravage the structure. One of the shortcuts was to forgo strong roof trusses necessary to support the Lodge from snow and wind. During the construction phase in the winter of 1913-14, much of the roof collapsed— an omen of the structural difficulties that would plague the Lodge.

While the Lodge was under construction, the first general superintendent and landscape engineer for the National Parks, Mark Daniels, consulted with Steel and Parkhurst and a development plan for the park—Rim Village—took shape. Daniels not only outlined priorities for National Park development, but as a private consultant, he drew up the plans for the Lodge's great hall.

Daniels' drawing shows an elaborate European great hall that offers a hint to what Crater Lake Lodge—the dream—was all about, but also shows additional interior supports that would have added to its structural stability. Knowing that there weren't funds for such a luxurious design, and once again ignoring the additional structural components, the great hall was simplified.

The scheduled 1912 opening turned into the summer of 1915, and when the doors finally opened, the Lodge was not exactly complete. Tar paper, not wood, covered the planned battened-board exterior, and fiberboard separated the rooms. Bathrooms were usually shared, and a generator provided erratic power. Yet the people came. If the rooms left much to be desired, the setting didn't. Visitors could find a seat at one of the great hall windows and gaze over the deep blue waters of Crater Lake. The massive fireplaces offered warmth, and the haven was certainly a step up from the tents still available.

But the honeymoon period was short, and tourists began complaining. Parkhurst struggled with the situation, and finally suggested that the government run the thing. By 1919, National Park Service Director Stephen Mather was furious, viewing Crater Lake Lodge as a blemish on the National Park Service's growing list of lodges. He didn't let up. In 1921, Parkhurst forfeited his lease, and Crater Lake Lodge Company, under the direction of Eric V. Hauser and Richard W. Price, took over the daunting task of running the Lodge, which was now practically blacklisted by officials who should have been promoting it.

Still the Lodge was not finished. The new concessionaires pumped money into upgrades and additions. The Lodge grew larger to accommodate the growing crowds who were finding their way to Crater Lake during the explosion in auto tourism. Fire escapes gripped the exterior, but the structural problems and bland interior remained much the same. Two annexes, in keeping with the stone, wood and windows of the main Lodge, were built. The project was completed in segments each summer, but twenty years later, rooms were still unfinished or unused.

While Lodge maintenance and improvement projects were foundering, in 1931-32, one of the largest building programs ever undertaken by the NPS was going on at Crater Lake National Park. The superintendent's residence (now the park headquarters and visitors' center), the naturalist's residence, rangers' dormitory and watchman lookout were a few of the projects that resulted and remain some of the finest examples of NPS rustic architecture in the West. These buildings not only benefited from more advanced engineering and design, but were built after the Park Service developed a highly stylized vision of what "parkitecture" should be.

Unfortunately, Crater Lake Lodge was suffering from the lack of such vision, funding and expertise. While the use of native materials—unpeeled logs, wood shingles and stone—was consistent with the idea that park buildings should blend with the environment, the Lodge, perched 1,000 feet above the rim, would always be an "eyesore" to the purists whose influence on NPS building was growing. By 1943, Park Superintendent E.P. Leavitt deemed it a "fire trap of the worst sort." In 1953, the NPS commissioned a report that recommended rehabilitation of the Lodge: the cost, $72,000. Price balked at the recommendation and sold the concession to Harry Smith and his son the following year. In 1959, the concession and building again changed hands, to

The wrath of historic preservationists and nostalgia-driven Oregonians was seriously underestimated. Saving Crater Lake Lodge became a cause to be reckoned with.

Opposite: The National Park Service added the back patio to the Lodge where guests can enjoy views of Crater Lake.

In 1917, the decor may have been Spartan, but guests were still enthralled by the Lodge and its setting.

Ralph Peyton and James Griffin. The NPS wanted to buy the Lodge and convert it into a visitor center and museum or demolish it. The concessionaire would then take the money and build a motel to accommodate guests. Finally, in 1967, the NPS bought the Lodge. But it was not destroyed or converted. It was leased back to Peyton and Griffin with a thirty-year contract. For nearly twenty years, the Lodge opened each summer amid mounting problems and controversy.

In 1980, a General Accounting Office report criticized not only the Lodge's safety problems, but also the drop in the number of overnight visitors. The next year, the Lodge was added to the National Register of Historic Places, making any changes or demolition of the Lodge a historic preservation issue. In 1984, following two decades of studies, the National Park Service recommended demolition and the construction of a new hotel

away from the rim. After surviving decades of brutal winter storms, sheltering thousands of visitors, enduring the indignities of "cosmetic" renovation and neglect, Crater Lake Lodge was in danger of being razed.

But the wrath of historic preservationists and nostalgia-driven Oregonians was seriously underestimated. Saving Crater Lake Lodge became a cause to be reckoned with. In 1984, the Historic Preservation League of Oregon officially began monitoring the National Park Service's plans for the now decrepit Lodge. The League challenged government reports and cost estimates for renovation in a position paper and began the fight. By 1987, the Oregon legislature passed a resolution to save the Lodge. During the fight, the Lodge continued to decay, and a report completed by consulting engineers in 1989 suggested that the Lodge's middle section, including the great hall

and guest rooms on the upper floors, might collapse of their own weight. Park Service Regional Director Charles Odegaard ordered the Lodge closed on May 26, 1989.

This was not the beginning of the end, but a respite before the Lodge's transformation. Only two years after Crater Lake Lodge's closure, reconstruction began. In these days of governmental budget-slashing, it stands as a symbol of what good can come of money well spent.

The rehabilitated four-story structure, with its forest-green roof and brown-shingled siding, built on a steel-reinforced foundation of native volcanic stone is a reminder of the past. The irony is that hardly any of the Lodge is old. For the historical architects working on the project, it was necessary to look at the design in a new light. Instead of a traditional historic restoration, this would be an "adaptive restoration" to evoke the feeling of what the Lodge should have been. The Portland architectural firm of Fletcher Farr Ayotte, whose original assignment was to design a new Lodge, switched gears.

"With most historic structures there is usually an event, a person or an architectural style which defines its historic significance. Crater Lake Lodge had none of those," explained David Wark, the firm's lead architect on the project. "What it did have was a history that came from people's emotional attachment."

The firm's framework for the project became "what feels right, what is emotionally right, and what is appropriate to the Lodge."

What didn't "feel right" was just about everything done since about 1930. Besides the structural problems, including huge cables running through the interior and hooked to facing walls that held the great hall together, and limestone mortar that

Far left: Views are spectacular seen from a claw-foot bathtub. The dining room in 1917, left, and the restored room, below, offer much the same rustic ambiance.

had turned to sand, there was the interior. Hideous carpets (twenty-two different patterns were found during the gutting process), tacky wine casks and bug zappers that festooned the dining room, a reception desk that blocked lake views, and uninviting guest rooms were all to be considered. At least the main floor hadn't always been that way, and historical photographs gave a blueprint to the rustic lodge simplicity that had long ago lost its dignity.

On May 1, 1991, Phase I began. Crews from Dale Ramsey Construction of Corvallis, Oregon, began to dismantle the great hall. Stone walls were taken apart, and fireplace stones were numbered for reconstruction in the great hall. New foundations for the great hall, lobby, dining room and kitchen were poured. (There had never been a foundation under the great hall and lobby.) A steel-beamed infrastructure was constructed, and carpenters framed the great hall. A Herculean body was completed, ready for the aging skin of stone and wood to cover the skeleton. All of the exterior walls, except the great hall, are a facade of original materials. The kitchen was gutted and replaced.

Stones that framed windows and doors were

The original Lodge never looked like this. After rehabilitation, it was decorated with many Gustav Stickley reproductions.

saved and put back in their original places. What was not replaced was reconfigured in the same rough character. The huge exterior stairway was removed. All entries or exits had to be incorporated into existing doors. Sixty-hour weeks were the norm, with winter breathing down the workers' necks. When construction was halted for the season, a centerpiece had been created.

Phase II lasted three summers. Emerick Construction Company of Salem, Oregon, got the contract for the remaining work. While the centerpiece was well underway, the unstable annex and annex wing were shored and stabilized with new foundations and support columns. All of the reconstruction had to meet seismic guidelines. The entire roof was replaced, including rafters and cedar shingles; the finished product can support snow loads of 350 pounds per square foot. While exterior work continued, attention turned to the interior.

That began at the entry. "There was no sense of arrival in the original design," noted Wark, "no orientation to the lake." Seeing the lake—the very reason for the Lodge's existence—became a hallmark for the interior plans and design. There are views everywhere—from the lobby, great hall and dining room, and from hallways that now serve as transition areas. By each elevator there is an alcove with a window seat and lake view.

The great hall has thirteen-foot-high beamed ceilings, unpeeled Douglas-fir log-paneled walls, and a huge fireplace rebuilt with the original stones and salvaged fir pillars and pieces of paneling. The dining room is elegant and comfortable, with two walls of windows, another rebuilt stone fireplace and Crater Lake Lodge china on the tables.

No two guest rooms are alike. Half of them feature views of the rim and lake, while the others face a panorama of other volcanic mountains. All have modern bathrooms, and the claw-foot bathtubs in former attic alcove rooms are perfect vantage points from which to watch the changing mountain skies. Historical photos of the park and Lodge lend richness to every room.

Edelman/Naiman designers of Portland selected interior furnishings to complement the new setting. As Carol Edelman recounted: "Before I started really digging, I looked at it as something like Timberline Lodge. A great era that kind of went bad." What she found was an interior design that was bad to the core. "This place never had anything. It was like camping in the wilderness inside a building instead of a tent. There were nice stone fireplaces, but not much else to talk about."

Understanding the heart and soul of the lodge experience was her cornerstone; from there, the interior designers concentrated on what the Lodge should have been and what the visitors thought they had experienced. Edelman saw it as an "extension of the spirit of out of doors inside." The result is an interior not caught at one point in time. The blend of Gustav Stickley reproductions, Mission, metal, log and twig furniture and accessories reflects continuation of what might have been done over time.

The "new" Lodge is managed by Crater Lake Company, a subsidiary of The Estey Corporation. The building is owned by the National Park Service and the Company maintains the Lodge under NPS direction.

Crater Lake Lodge, the elegant idea of another era, is finally a reality. The architects, historians, contractors and designers took nostalgia and a decaying old Lodge and gave them new life. As one historian noted, "It's glorified history—history without the smells."

The transformation of the great hall drew from a variety of styles: "I wanted to create what should have evolved over time," explained decorator Carol Edelman.

Crater Lake is one of nature's great surprises. Wizard Island pokes through the deep blue water, and Crater Lake Lodge is barely visible in the distance.

Paradise Inn

Historic Time Capsule

The National Park Service was struggling for its stamp of congressional approval when Stephen T. Mather, then assistant to the Secretary of the Interior and future director of the NPS, visited Mount Rainier National Park in July 1915. Mather had climbed Mount Rainier for the first time in 1905, so he appreciated the grandeur of the peak. A decade later, the visit was not a mountaineering expedition, but part of a sweeping trip of the parks taken by him, his assistant Horace Albright, and a rotating group of influential men.

Mount Rainier National Park, established in 1899, was the fifth such designated park in the country. With the glaciated dome of the stratovolcano rising 14,411 feet above the lush Northwestern forests, and visitors within easy access from Tacoma and Seattle, Mather knew the park needed better accommodations. A variety of individuals owned and operated facilities such as Longmire's lodge near the park entrance, and John Reese's tent lodging in Paradise Valley. Mather took a look at the operations and was not pleased. Besides a more cohesive management of existing facilities, Mather wanted a Great Lodge in the Paradise Valley with views of Mount Rainier and the Tatoosh Range.

He brought together a group of Tacoma and Seattle businessmen, and while on an eighty-five-mile pack trip around Mount Rainier, Mather and Albright began the campaign to form the Rainier

National Park Company. On March 1, 1916, a charter for incorporation was taken out, and T.H. Martin was made general manager. The company eventually bought out both the National Park and Longmire Springs Hotel operations at Longmire and John Reese's camp operation at Paradise.

The idea of a luxury hotel in the park was nothing new. In 1911, Tacoma architect Frederick Heath proposed a $2 million dollar "dream project" for a 400-room hotel featuring a glass observatory, four wings, a sanitarium, natatorium, club house, tennis courts, gardens and its own power plant to

be built near the park's entrance at Longmire with access to the natural mineral springs. The plans were presented to the Tacoma Commercial Club and Chamber of Commerce where Commercial Club manager T.H. Martin began drumming up support from a skeptical audience.

The idea languished, but apparently not Martin's enthusiasm. As the Rainier National Park Company took shape—with Martin in charge—new architectural drawings were being done by Heath & Gove. By the summer of 1915, Frederick Heath's initial "dream" plan had been scaled down and the site moved to Paradise Valley. According to Tacoma newspaper accounts, John Reese initially agreed to build a $40,000 hotel at his tent camp, but National Park officials wanted Reese out of the picture. Reese balked at initial hotel plans saying the structure would not only cost from $350,000 to $400,000, but was not suited to the site and snow conditions. Mr. Reese was no match for Stephen Mather and was being edged out of the Mount Rainier National Park concession operations.

Drawings and stories of the proposed Paradise Inn ran in the Tacoma newspapers on February 13, 1916. On March 28, Frederick Heath officially unveiled drawings to the Board of Directors of the two-week old Rainier National Park Company. The newspaper illustration showed a three-winged building with a cylindrical center topped by a cone-

LOCATION: Mount Rainier National Park, Washington
OPENED: July 1, 1917
ARCHITECT: Heath & Gove, Tacoma, Washington; Paradise Annex (1920), Harlan Thomas
HISTORIC DESIGNATION: National Historic Landmark, May 28, 1987

69

shaped roof. The Inn would have a great hall with a two-and-a-half-story ceiling and an equally large dining room. Guest rooms would be above the dining room with a kitchen wing to the north. A three-story wing on the east side and one on the south side would have additional guest rooms, baths and suites. The majority of the guests would be housed in bungalow tents on the grounds.

Native material, most notably weathered timbers salvaged from a burn area known as the Silver Forest on the slopes of Mount Rainier, cedar shingles and native rock masonry were used, creating a building that blends with the environment, and one in keeping with what would evolve into the National Park Service's style of rustic architecture. The stone-and-glass cylindrical center was eliminated from the plan, resulting in a more subdued look reminiscent of Robert Reamer's 1906 design of Old Faithful Inn at Yellowstone. While Paradise Inn's pitched gable roof is only three stories compared to Old Faithful's seven-story Old House, both buildings are dominated by their roof designs.

The Inn was built during the summer and fall of 1916. According to Mount Rainier superintendent's 1916 Annual Report, heavy winter snow delayed construction. Luckily, some of the building material for the structure had been hauled to the site the previous fall, so while the roads were closed to automobile traffic until August 25, foundation work still began on July 20; timbers went up a month later. Additional supplies were hauled over the horse trail from Narada Falls to Paradise Valley until the road was cleared.

Workers set the naturally weathered Alaska-cedar logs in a rock foundation, creating a post and beam frame. Cedar shingles cover the exterior, and the original plan was to let them weather to match the Silver Forest cedar timbers and to paint

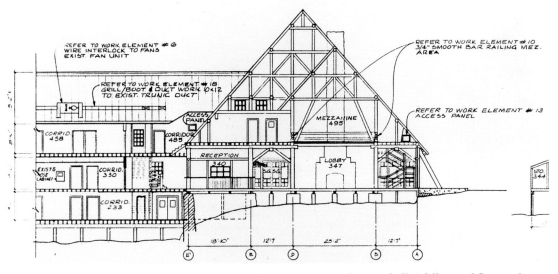

Top: Log timber columns support the dining room in the same way as in the great hall. A full second floor with guest rooms was added, covering the dining room's open rafters. Above: A contemporary section-drawing shows the intricate roof-bracing system of Paradise Inn.

the roof. The company proposed painting the roof red, but National Park Service landscape architect Charles Punchard vetoed the idea, opting for dark green. A three-level guest wing was added on the east side soon after the main building was completed; most rooms had shared baths. The Inn opened on schedule July 1, 1917, having cost $100,000.

For the first month of operation, snow blocked the road and cars couldn't reach the Inn. That didn't stop guests, who made the trek to the hotel by sleighs, snowshoes or on horseback. Waterproof boots were made available for men and women who wanted to hike in, according to the park superintendent's report.

Their reward was a chance to lounge in the 50- by 112-foot great hall in front of one of two massive fireplaces, take their meals in the equally impressive dining room, then adjourn to simple sleeping quarters.

Over the years, alterations and decorative painting have changed some of the detail of the great hall, but it retains the grandeur of its early days. Light streams in from the dormer windows high above the mezzanine, highlighting the repetitive structural framework with posts, beams and trusses that mark the architectural signature of the great hall. Iron rungs grip the cedar poles, added to reinforce the splitting timbers, and a system of cables and metal bracing helps support the building against the onslaught of heavy snow. During the 1920s, additional cedar beams were added to create a permanent brace against the snow.

Alaskan cedar shaped andirons hold burning logs in the four- by six-foot fireplaces made from locally quarried stone. Hand-painted forest and icicle designs, done sometime in the 1930s, decorate the huge cedar poles. The parquet floor (not original) is polished to a high gloss.

The snow-covered Paradise Inn may appear picturesque in this historical photograph, but the annual damage done to the structure creates ongoing problems.

In 1925, Inn manager Paul Sceva added the mezzanine that circles the great hall from the second-floor level. Natural light pours through the dormers, and hickory tables and chairs—many original—fill the space. This is an ideal getaway spot to read, write or drink tea while observing the goings-on below. It is also a good place to get a close look at the joinery work. According to Sceva's memoirs, these were originally hand-notched; snow loads that were slowly crushing the huge structure required the addition of bolts and bracing.

The Japanese lanterns and rustic triangular log fixtures that originally hung from the ceiling were replaced in the 1930s by lights with parchment shades decorated with paintings of wild flowers done by Inn employees. In 1989, Dale C. Thompson painted the current conical shades with

such themes as "bunchberry dogwood," "monarch butterfly" and "alpine autumn." There are five sizes of shades, and smaller versions run along the balcony ceiling. Above the floral lights are original cone-shaped light fixtures hanging like so many belfry bats. When it came to furnishing the Inn, the first batch of furniture was salvaged from the Stratford Hotel in Tacoma, scheduled for demolition and owned by a member of the Rainier National Park Company Board of Directors. The board got a "deal" on the Arts and Crafts style furniture, but the Inn deserved more.

Enter Hans Fraehnke. Much of the handmade furniture at Paradise Inn has long been attributed to this German carpenter. Not until 1996, when Sarah Allaback wrote *The Rustic Furnishings of Mount Rainier National Park, 1916-1996* for the Historic American Buildings Survey were the de-

Hans Fraehnke's fourteen-foot-tall grandfather clock seems to hold court over the great hall.

tails known. In 1949, The *Tacoma Ledger* described how Fraehnke hiked to Paradise each March for seven successive seasons to work there through November. He also had a workshop in Fife. This refutes the long-standing story that he created his furniture in one *very* long season.

The distinctive furniture began to appear in the Inn after the first season, beginning with one of the massive fourteen-foot Alaskan-cedar split-log tables and followed by a pair of throne chairs. If Fraehnke wasn't building furniture, he was customizing anything ordinary at the Inn. He covered the front and sides of the registration desk with cedar, put cedar posts with triangular wood caps between the clerk's windows and designed the mailbox to look like a log stump. Fraehnke's most interesting transformation was turning a standard upright piano into a rustic piece of art. It was at this piano that President Harry Truman played a few tunes during a surprise 1945 visit. Perhaps the most impressive of Fraehnke's designs is the fourteen-foot-tall grandfather clock presiding over the Paradise Inn great hall. The clock, made in three sections, is topped with whittled post points as are the piano and some of the throne chairs.

When the Inn opened, Fraehnke's cedar furnishings were accompanied by beautiful hickory chairs, tables and settees from the Old Hickory Company of Indiana. Although the Stratford Hotel furniture was replaced, the massive cedar furniture and many of the original hickory pieces remain in Paradise Inn. Much of the original furniture at other Great Lodges disappeared over time; perhaps Hans Fraehnke built his pieces not only to last, but to stay put. The huge tables weigh 1,500 pounds, and it is unlikely that the throne chairs (from five to six feet high) would fit anywhere else.

The dining room furniture is not original, but the feel of the room has changed little since the first guests broke bread there. Diners enter through French doors from the great hall, down four steps into the one-and-one-half-story, 51- by 105-foot room. The dining room may have nearly the same floor space as the great hall, but it, along with the kitchen, is set back from the great hall wing with a slightly lower roofline. Exposed log timbers with beams and trusses add to the room's interest. A fifty-foot-high stone fireplace fills the north wall. Windows bank the length of the room. The triangular log light fixtures are original, perhaps moved from the great hall. Reproductions of the wild-flower lanterns hang along the side. The addition of waiter stations at each column is the only significant change to the room, where tables and chairs are lined up in perfect order.

In 1920, with guests shunning the tent cabins that surrounded Paradise Inn, the four-story Paradise Annex was built. Designed by Rainier National Park Company architect Harlan Thomas, the annex featured one hundred rooms, fifty-eight with private baths. Had the Heath & Gove original plans with a cylindrical hub been executed, the annex would have been accessed off the hub. Instead, only one wing was built and the annex originally stood alone. A later addition of a three-level "tunnel" or breezeway from the east wing connected the annex to the main building. Exposed log framing was proposed for the exterior, but never added.

The additions to Paradise Inn thrilled the traveling public. With the end of World War I, Americans turned to travel. The Milwaukee Railway dropped guests off in Ashford where Rainier National Park Company hired fourteen buses to shuttle them into the park. (The company sought railroad investment in their ventures, but was never successful.) By 1924, all park visitation and

Andirons shaped like Alaskan cedar trees, above left, fill the fireplace openings. Rustic cedar "throne" chairs, left, and an upright piano, once played by President Harry Truman, above right, were designed by Hans Fraehnke.

Opposite: The 50- by 112-foot great hall, with its repetitive post and beam design has had structural supports and a mezzanine added, but seems as grand as the day it opened.

For the first month of operation, snow blocked the road and cars couldn't reach the Inn. That didn't stop the guests, who made the trek to the hotel by sleigh, snowshoe, or on horseback.

RNP Co. records had been broken. The company was making a profit; the combined guest count for Paradise Inn, National Park Inn and the cabins reached 1,500 each weekend, according to park records.

As more visitors came, their tastes and demands for first-rate accommodations increased. Tent cabins were taken down and housekeeping cabins constructed. The company installed water in the main rooms, refurnished the guest rooms in the annex and hoped for the best. In 1931, they even built a golf course. The concessionaire also promoted skiing. Ski competition, carnivals and tournaments were held during the 1930s, and in 1936-37, the company opened the Inn for the winter season. A portable ski tow was installed.

Many of the changes at Paradise Inn came while Paul Sceva, who managed and promoted Paradise Inn for forty-six years, was in charge. Sceva suggested the replacement of most of the original peaked and gabled dormers—ruined by snow loads—with shed dormers. In 1935, he also recommended the demolition and replacement of the original kitchen and the addition of the gift shop on the west side of the lobby plus enlargement of the lobby porch. Sceva sold the housekeeping cabins around the Inn, and in the end, lobbied on behalf of RNP Co. for the government to buy the company's holdings.

World War II brought a decline in visitors to Mount Rainier. The Inn continued operation under rationing regulations and with a small staff through the war years. In 1942-43, the U.S. Army used the facilities for troops testing mountain travel, food and equipment, and training for winter mountain conditions. After the war, the Park Service did an inventory and appraisal of the buildings at Paradise. Time and winter had taken their toll. The failing Rainier National Park Company sold Paradise Inn to the National Park Service in 1952, and the Park Service, in turn, contracted with concessionaires to operate the Inn.

In the 1960s, the National Park Service proposed demolishing the Inn. Public uproar was immediate. In response, the NPS budgeted $1.75 million to restore the Inn in 1979. Today, Mt. Rainier Guest Services, a subsidiary of Guest Services, Inc., manages the hotels, food services and souvenir stores. GSI maintains the interior and grounds of the Inn. The Park Service is responsible for the exterior as well as the basic structure of the building. A 1996 Structural Engineering Study is the basis for ongoing structural repairs paid for through the use of franchise fees paid by GSI.

Caring for a national landmark is an endless responsibility. For instance, the post, beam and truss structure with the pitched gable roof was meant to withstand the tons of snow that buried the building each winter. Unfortunately, the tremendous lateral crush of snow and ice on the uphill side of the building has played havoc with the design. For eighty years, engineers, architects and contractors have been trying to reinforce the structure. The original solid log columns that protrude from under the eaves along the exterior were replaced with steel reinforced versions, placed at more of an angle to help support the building.

Other major rehabilitation of the Inn, including a lateral restraint system, new floor systems, repair to the roofs and windows occurred in the 1950s and 1970s. Upgrading of the fire protection system, foundation stabilization, additional window replacement, reroofing and exterior painting are on the new list. Any major rehabilitation requires acquiring additional congressional funding.

While the smaller National Park Inn in the

The huge dining room is almost as large as the Inn's great hall.

historic Longmire District near the park entrance was totally renovated in 1989-90, Paradise Inn and annex are caught in a time warp. That is not to say that the grandeur of the Inn has vanished.

Mount Rainier National Park celebrates its centennial in 1999. Some of the park's rich history is found in Paradise Inn, where visitors will likely marvel at the fabulous great hall and dining room

and enjoy tea on the mezzanine. Still, even with a fresh coat of paint, the exterior of the building will always seem rather simple set against the huge dome of Mount Rainier. Perhaps that was how it was always meant to be.

Bryce Canyon Lodge was built of locally harvested timber and quarried stone. Soon after it opened, Gilbert Stanley Underwood began additions that transformed the Lodge into an architecturally significant example of rustic park architecture.

A Complete Architectural Experience

Bryce Canyon Lodge is a bigger story than that of one lodge complex. The Union Pacific (UP) system saw potential in extending railroad lines into the little-known environs of southern Utah and developing tourism in the state's parks. The grand plan would bring tourists by rail to a main station and then shuttle them by motor coaches on a "Loop Tour," where they could take in the beauty of Cedar Breaks, Zion National Park, Bryce Canyon and eventually Kaibab Forest and the North Rim of the Grand Canyon. Along the way, they would stay at Union Pacific constructed lodges and dine at its restaurants.

In late 1922, the railroad outlined a $5 million plan that included the construction of two branch lines and lodging for the Cedar City, Zion and Bryce sites and a smaller facility at Cedar Breaks. Not only would the lines open up the spectacular canyons of Zion and pink limestone formations of Bryce, it would provide transportation lines for agricultural products, coal and other ore from the region. Perhaps most important to the competitive Union Pacific railmen was the potential of drawing the highly successful tourist trade from the Santa Fe Railway at the South Rim, and duplicating the Northern Pacific's success at Yellowstone National Park.

The obstacles to development of this region began with its relative obscurity. Early Mormon settlers were more concerned with the daily challenges of survival than with the spectacular beauty around them. J.W. Humphrey, Forest Service supervisor for the region, reluctantly visited Bryce Canyon in 1915 and was so taken with the specta-

cle that he made it a personal campaign to open the area to the public. He hired photographers and brought the beauty of the region to the attention of the railroad companies. In 1918, the first newspaper account of the wonders of Bryce Canyon ran in the Sunday *Salt Lake Tribune*. The article, "Utah's New Wonderland," was the benchmark for the beginning of southern Utah's tourist trade, and later became one of UP's promotional slogans.

Two years earlier, Ruby and Minnie Syrett had decided to homestead near Bryce Canyon and selected a site a few miles from what is now Sunset Point. After the publication of "Utah's New Won-

derland," tourists began arriving to see for themselves the exquisitely eroded amphitheater sculpted through the arid southern Utah landscape. The Syretts were soon pitching tents and preparing meals for the first visitors. The Syretts built Tourist's Rest, a rough-sawn log building and cabins on the future site of Bryce Canyon Lodge. Eventually, the UP bought them out for $10,000.

Once the UP settled on the "loop" plan, the challenges for completing the project were huge. Road access to the parks, forests and monuments was miserable, and the water situation unreliable. After securing concession contracts to the parks and monument areas and confirmation that the roads would be improved, the UP constructed a rail spur from Lund, Utah, to Cedar City, where a new depot was built; in 1923, they opened El Escalante Hotel in Cedar City.

In 1924, a dining pavilion at Cedar Breaks and Zion Lodge opened; Bryce Canyon Lodge opened the following year. Additions were constructed on Bryce and Zion in 1926-27. In 1928, Grand Canyon Lodge was completed on the North Rim. One architect was responsible for all of this work—Gilbert Stanley Underwood. With each plan, Underwood refined his approach to rustic architecture. He drew from the Arts and Crafts

LOCATION: Bryce Canyon National Park, Utah
OPENED: May 15, 1925
ARCHITECT: Gilbert Stanley Underwood
HISTORIC DESIGNATION: National Historic Landmark, May 28, 1987

style that influenced the National Park Service and developed elements that he would repeat throughout his career. Each successive lodge became more dramatic, its details more elegant.

While early railroad lodge projects had often been built prior to the formation of the National Park Service, by the time the Utah project at Zion began, they were closely supervised by the Park Service and its director, Stephen T. Mather. Mather was not exactly enthusiastic about the Utah parks, in part because of the agency's small budget and staff, but once he committed to overseeing the Zion National Park project, he set high standards and a tough approval process for structures in the parks.

Mather and Daniel Hull, NPS landscape engineer, rejected the UP architect's first Zion plans. According to Underwood's biographer, Joyce Zaitlin, Hull suggested to his friend and professional colleague that the young architect apply for the job. It was a suggestion that would have an impact on both National Park architecture and the future career of Underwood. Underwood, who had just opened his office in Los Angeles, was familiar with the NPS, and was working on plans for the Yosemite Village post office (plans rejected by Mather).

Underwood met UP executives in Omaha, then joined a party surveying the site for Zion, continuing on to Bryce Canyon. The two settings offered opposite opportunities: Zion was in the canyon surrounded by towering cliffs, while Bryce would be on the Paunsaugunt Plateau, one-eighth mile from the rim of the spectacular pink-hued hoodoos of the canyon. Here was the young architect's opportunity to draw not only from his Harvard education, but from nature.

Underwood's first design for Zion was also rejected, but the architect retooled it to fit Mather's idea of a smaller main pavilion, with large stone pillars, and cabins. All of the "loop" facilities would offer accommodations for a wide range of visitors with varying economic means.

The lodge site at Bryce Canyon was clearly less spectacular, set at the edge of a small grove of

Below: Gilbert Stanley Underwood's 1924 front-elevation drawing for the Union Pacific system shows the Lodge's original simple design. Opposite, lower: The addition of cornerstone piers, a gift shop and auditorium gave the Lodge, pictured in 1937, the rustic appearance favored by the National Park Service. Opposite, top: Guests gather around the radio by the tour desk soon after the Lodge opened in 1925. Note the hammered-copper fireplace hood.

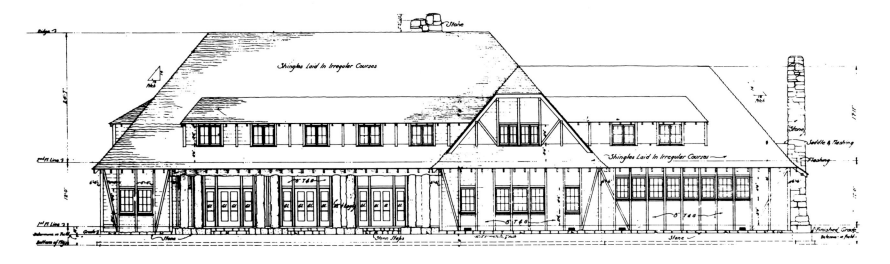

ponderosa pines. The rim was within walking distance, but visitors had no idea what awaited them a short walk from the Lodge. The UP purchased a portion of the site from the state and leased additional land from the Forest Service. Then, under pressure from Mather, in March of 1923, the UP spun off a subsidiary, Utah Parks Company (UPC), to develop and operate the railroad's "loop" resort operations. All the while, Utah Senator Reed Smoot was introducing various bills to protect the Bryce Canyon area. Bryce Canyon became a National Monument in 1923. In 1927, UPC deeded its land to the U.S. government in return for a concession

agreement and road improvements—the Zion–Mt. Carmel road—paving the way for Bryce Canyon to become a National Park on February 25, 1928.

With the park's status in limbo, work continued at the site. UPC decided to use local timber and stone for construction. Rather than bring massive logs by rail from the Northwest, as had been done at El Tovar and Glacier National Park lodges, the Lodge and cabins were constructed of local materials—small, milled lumber and logs. Not only did UPC officials want to save money, but they were interested in securing the support of the local community, and hiring local laborers was part of that plan. They signed a contract in the spring of 1923 with Ruby Syrett and Owen Orton to harvest timber.

Stone was quarried about one-and-a-half miles from the site. The railway wanted stone walls built "up to the snow line," feeling the timber was of "inferior quality," but Underwood's March 1924 elevation drawings indicate only stone foundation, chimneys and steps. In fact, the steps were built with brick and most of the stone facade that now defines the Lodge was added later.

Some historians think that the Lodge was meant as a temporary structure, to be used until the UPC could get permission to build on the edge of the rim. That would explain the simplicity of the original exposed-frame structure. Pairs of twenty-inch log columns supporting the portico along the front of the Lodge, and a sweeping, wood-shingled, gable roof with shed dormer windows were the only exceptional details of the exterior. Underwood's plans called for shingles to be "laid in irregular course." (The undulating pattern of shingles continues to be replicated with each new roof.) The original portion of the Lodge, finished for the 1925 summer season, included a lobby with information desk, post office, kitchen and dining

room with guest rooms above the lobby and dining rooms. Bath facilities were on both floors.

Inside, a beautiful hammered-copper hood over the roughly quarried stone fireplace in the lobby, and log and incandescent light bulb chandeliers gave the room—filled with hickory furniture—the requisite "lodge" feel.

In 1925, the Union Pacific began its advertising campaign: "America's Most Enchanting Vacation Land—Now Open. Here in Southern Utah are canyons preserving the flaming sunsets of a million years! Mountains of vermilion! Vast amphitheatres of filigreed stone stained with uncounted colors and studded with jewelled statues! Cathedrals, castles, pyramids, temples! Nowhere else are scenes so marvelous as in Zion National Park, Bryce Canyon–Cedar Breaks."

The first tourist season was a success beyond UPC President C.R. Gray's expectations. In October 1925, he outlined a request to the Union Pacific in Omaha to build additional tourist facilities at both Zion and Bryce that would nearly double the Lodge facilities. "In this season of three months we handled an aggregate of 1,847 rail passengers, and I am informed that this is a larger number than was handled by rail the first year after the line was opened to West Yellowstone, and we have occasion to feel that is an auspicious beginning," Gray noted the following month in a proposal to Omaha.

If the Lodge was meant to be temporary, plans to build another lodge on the rim never materialized. Underwood began a series of expansion plans, and Bryce Canyon Lodge was transformed. In 1927, a gift shop, soda fountain and barber shop were added on the south end of the building and the front portico extended along the addition. The following year, an auditorium was added to the southwest. Both rooms featured open ceilings with

Opposite: The rehabilitation of Bryce Canyon Lodge in the late 1980s transformed the lobby, by then stripped of its history, by reproducing many of the elements lost over time. That included the lobby's log light fixtures, originally designed by the architect, and the outside lanterns, above.

Opposite: The dining room was part of the extensive rehabilitation at Bryce. Light fixtures were forged based on original designs.

In addition to the Lodge, Underwood designed log-and-stone Deluxe Cabins. Once decorated with fiber weave furniture and rugs, fires still glow (now fueled by gas), and guests enjoy much of the cabins' original atmosphere.

scissor trusses, horizontal wood paneling, and wood floors. A huge stone fireplace occupies the south wall of the auditorium, and a panel of nearly floor-to-ceiling windows still fills the west wall. The dining room and kitchen were doubled in size, a basement was added under the kitchen expansion and bath facilities were expanded. The wings not only added much needed space, but created a charming center courtyard. Outside, large cornerstone piers gave not only rustic detail but a feeling of substance to the structure. A final touch, a sign with letters made of branches, "Bryce Canyon Lodge," still hangs today.

Next to the Lodge, a complex of sixty-seven wood-frame standard and economy cabins housed guests, and by 1929, fifteen Deluxe Cabins were finished. The ten duplex and five quadruplex Deluxe Cabins reflect the rustic design the architect was fine-tuning, each featuring a steeply pitched gable roof, stone foundation and chimney, log-framed porches and half-log-slab exterior walls.

Underwood was hitting his stride. As his office continued to provide plans for additional buildings for the Utah Parks, Mather was looking for an architect to build a major hotel at Yosemite National Park. The Ahwahnee hotel would be Underwood's most famous NPS project (see page 91). But his work for UPC was not finished. In 1927, after the UPC finally got approval for a lodge and cabins on the North Rim of the Grand Canyon at Bright Angel Point, they again turned to Underwood. The company was pleased with the architect's work and both the NPS and railroad wanted to expand on Underwood's style throughout the "loop."

Grand Canyon Lodge was built on the very rim of the canyon, with guests housed in cabins nearby. The limestone, ponderosa log and log-slab sided Lodge seemed an extension of the eroded rim of the canyon itself. A two-story semicircular sunroom with plate glass windows, outdoor terraces, watchtower and floor-to-ceiling dining room windows all offered unparalleled views. The Lodge and cabins opened for the 1928 season with accommodations for 250 guests. "It harmonizes perfectly with its sublime surroundings and seems itself a work of nature," read one UP brochure. But there was more than advertising hype. The park superintendent wrote in his annual report that the Lodge's completion was "one of the most important steps in the history of the Park." A combination of Underwood's Park Service rustic design, and no doubt the influence of Mary Colter's work on the South Rim of the Grand Canyon, it was a masterpiece.

On September 1, 1932, the Lodge burned in the largest structural fire in Grand Canyon's history. Two years later, the UPC began rebuilding the Lodge on the remaining stone foundation, but there is no evidence that Underwood took part designing the "new" Lodge. All but two of the Deluxe Cabins survived the fire, and were redecorated in the mid-1990s in keeping with the original decor. While the rebuilt Lodge is stunning, the watchtower was eliminated, and the jagged rooflines that blended so perfectly with the rim of the canyon were replaced with a traditional pitched roof.

Of all Underwood's UPC work, Bryce Canyon Lodge and Deluxe Cabins is the only project that remains intact. Zion Park Lodge burned in 1966, and the pavilion at Cedar Breaks is gone. Zion Lodge was rebuilt on the original footprint, and has been updated, but it reflects little of Underwood's original design although his cabins still stand. At Bryce Canyon visitors can enjoy an "Underwood" experience. While his standard cabins and most of the housekeeping cabins were removed, the Bryce Inn, now used as a Camp Store, is also an Underwood design. That is not to say the Lodge itself has not been altered. The hammered-copper fireplace hood was removed and the fireplace rebuilt probably the same year the Lodge opened. The second version does not have the keyhole design of the other Lodge fireplaces; instead, a huge stone lintel can be seen under a polished copper hood. Minor alterations continued through the 1930s to meet the needs of park visitors.

The park was closed for two years during World War II, then experienced a postwar boom. The 1950s roared in with tourists overloading the facilities. Exterior changes were made to accommodate the huge influx of cars, and the water and sewer systems were updated. Bathrooms were remodeled and fire escapes added. The other "improvements" included painting the exterior bright yellow and adding awnings over the windows. The barber shop and soda fountain were removed. Linoleum was laid over the tongue-and-grove wood floors, acoustic tiles covered the original wood ceilings and clusters of saucer-shaped fixtures replaced the log chandeliers. Space heaters were suspended from the beams. The changes were made in an effort to update the structures and meet the demands of the NPS and public. By 1980, according to park preservation crew personnel, almost all of the interior detail was gone.

The summer train line discontinued service in 1960. UPC struggled through the 1960s, and in 1972, the company that built most of the facilities at Zion, Cedar Breaks, North Rim and Bryce Canyon dissolved, donating its massive holdings to the National Park Service. TW Recreational Services, Inc., continues to manage the properties; however, in December 1995, TW was purchased by AmFac Parks and Resorts, Inc.

Gilbert Stanley Underwood's stunning Grand Canyon Lodge opened in 1928 as part of the Union Pacific's "loop" tour, below. In 1932, the limestone and ponderosa masterpiece was reduced to smoldering ash and its stone foundation. It was rebuilt eliminating the watchtower, instead opting for a standard pitched roof, left.

In 1986, Bryce Canyon Lodge experienced a renaissance when a joint venture between the concessionaire (TW Recreational Services) and the National Park Service began. The rehabilitation of the Lodge was part of the "Partners in Preservation" project. Behind the plywood paneling, acoustic ceilings, carpet and linoleum, the historic structure of Bryce Canyon Lodge still lived. In the fall of 1988, work began on the first phase—rehabilitation of the ground floor. Unfortunately, the temporary intent of the original Lodge came back to haunt those who were rehabilitating it. According to NPS project supervisor Kevin Brandt, the foundation "was virtually nonexistent." The crew lifted the entire building and put a true structural perimeter around it. Once the building was on firm foundation, other work began. The goal was to keep the spirit of the building and its historic integrity while meeting new building code requirements.

Not only had the lobby lost its historical charm, it also suffered from overcrowding as dinner guests waited to be seated. Part of the plan reconfigured

Underwood used exposed trusses for the roof of the Bryce Canyon Lodge auditorium addition, a style he favored. The massive stone fireplace, tongue-and-groove wood flooring and wooden-cross light fixtures are all original.

the space to include a waiting area outside of the dining room, thus freeing up the lobby. Public bathrooms were moved and access to the center courtyard opened up. The registration desk was moved back and the lobby space restored to vintage 1926. The bracketed wood columns supporting four twelve-inch-wide wood beams were reinforced with concrete bases, and vertical-grain Douglas-fir finished the walls and ceiling. The log light fixtures were reproduced according to Underwood's design and hung from the rafters.

The auditorium had not suffered from earlier "improvements and modernization." The hardwood floor is original, and the exposed wood ceiling with scissor trusses, rafters and purlins are stained dark brown to give the room a woodsy feel. Six cast-iron chandeliers were refurbished during the renovation.

The wood and glass post office was meticulously removed during the work, then replaced and the wood refinished. The gift shop has the same open ceiling with scissor trusses as found in the auditorium, but the ceiling has been painted white, and the old soda fountain, once under the second floor balcony, is gone.

As reported in the *1985 Bryce Canyon Lodge Historic Structures Report,* "Perhaps of all the main public spaces of the building, the historic character of the dining room has been the most altered." When rehabilitation began, plywood paneling covered the walls, acoustic panels filled the ceiling, and pot and candle light fixtures hung from it. The two stone fireplaces and cracked trusses were all that was visible. After analyzing weight and snow loads, the crew replaced side columns with steel and covered them with wood facades; flat timber trusses were reinforced with steel plates and bolts, and repro-

Gilbert Stanley Underwood also designed Zion Park Lodge and Cabins as part of his work for the Union Pacific. The lodge burned in 1966 and was rebuilt on the same footing. The stone pillars, meant to reflect the pinnacles of the area, are reminiscent of the original design. Jeff and Alexa Henry

ductions of cast-iron single light fixtures now hang throughout the room.

The second story of the Lodge had gone through various phases. First used for guests, it later housed female employees in dormitory quarters. Suitors once filled the courtyard below to talk with their girlfriends and the women used to climb onto the roof to sunbathe. All of that is history. While the first-floor renovation is in keeping with the original appearance, the upper story was gutted and made into guest suites and offices. The rooms are sunny, with white painted walls and mauve carpeting. Even the wicker furniture (the Lodge and cabins were originally furnished with natural-colored fiber furniture) is painted white. While the guest rooms have no historic signifi-

cance, each door has a brass plaque with the name of some figure from Bryce Canyon's past.

The few remaining standard cabins along the main walkway on the front of the Lodge were renovated, circa 1949, for employee housing. The Deluxe cabins, found in clusters by the main Lodge have been remodeled over the years. The charming fiber tables, chairs and desks with cross-pattern weaving, and printed fiber rugs are gone or warehoused, but the stone fireplaces still glow (albeit with gas jets), highlighting the exposed beam ceilings that give the cabins much of their character. Guests can step out on the front porches, run a hand across the original log railings, and take a deep breath of clear air, then walk to the rim of Bryce Canyon, and gaze at the wonder of another National Park.

The Ahwahnee rises in perfect unity with the surrounding granite walls. Balconies, varied rooflines and rough-cut stone are elements that add to its architectural success.

Rustic Elegance Against a Granite Backdrop

Naturalist/conservationist John Muir and National Park Service Director Stephen T. Mather were both passionate about Yosemite National Park. In 1868, when John Muir laid eyes on Yosemite Valley, he experienced an epiphany. The towering granite formations, valley and powerful waterfalls were his vision of heaven on Earth. Muir and Robert Underwood Johnson, editor of *Century* magazine, were instrumental in the establishment of Yosemite National Park, finalized on October 1, 1890. While on a 1912 camping trip in the Sierra, Muir—well into his seventies—met Mather. It was during this chance meeting that the famed naturalist lobbied the well-to-do businessman and mountaineering buff to devote his talents to saving the National Parks. In December 1914, the same month that Muir died, a reluctant, forty-seven-year-old Mather arrived at the nation's capital. Two years later, the National Park Service was born and Mather became its director.

Mather loved the stellar beauty of the park, and now, as NPS director, he saw an opportunity. Among his numerous challenges, here in his favorite park, he envisioned a cohesive, stylized park building program that would include a Great Lodge. It was Mather's firm belief that bringing those of wealth and influence to Yosemite and other National Parks would provide the future support, and thus congressional funding to pre-

serve them. And such guests needed a place to stay to appreciate the wilds surrounding them.

Those who first knew the beauty of the region were members of the Miwok tribe, who hunted, fished and gathered acorns in one of natures most

spectacular breadbaskets. Their peaceful days of summer encampments in the valley they called Ah-wah-ni or "large gaping mouth" were numbered. In

1851, a battalion of pioneer volunteers, in search of Indians accused of harassing miners and settlers along the lower Merced River, "discovered" the valley. Tourists infiltrated the region in 1855; a year later, the first permanent hotel was operating. In 1864, Yosemite Valley and the Mariposa Grove of Giant Sequoias were deeded to the state of California for protection as a "grant." Eventually, with the help of John Muir and President Theodore Roosevelt, those 48.6 acres were transferred from the state's control and included in Yosemite National Park.

By the time the National Park Service was established, private interests were entrenched at Yosemite. Tent camps, horse stables, stores, hotels and taverns haphazardly dotted the park. The old Sentinel Hotel, built in 1876, was the main hostelry in the valley. The State constructed the Stoneman House, but it burned in 1896. In 1916, Mather helped arrange for D.J. Desmond's construction of Yosemite Lodge. But there was still nothing suitable for guests accustomed to the finer things in life.

Mather needed a savvy, solid company to upgrade the park's operations and accommodations. As with other parks, his plan was to consolidate the major competing concession operators. At Yosemite, it was a particularly complex and difficult task. Among other things, he had to convince

LOCATION: Yosemite National Park, California
OPENED: July 14, 1927
ARCHITECT: Gilbert Stanley Underwood
HISTORIC DESIGNATION: National Historic Landmark, May 28, 1987

Yosemite National Park Superintendent W.B. Lewis, Yosemite Park and Curry Co. Board of Directors President A.B.C. Dohrmann, NPS landscape engineer Tom Vint, Yosemite Park and Curry Co. President Don Tresidder, and architect Gilbert Stanley Underwood hold Underwood's rendering of the hotel that would cover most of old Kenneyville.

Below: Underwood continued to downscale the hotel. This rendering, dated 1926, is still larger than what was finally built.

Opposite: The Ahwahnee seen from the four-mile trail on the South Rim. Keith Walklet

Jenny "Mother" Curry, the successful owner of Curry Company. Finally, in 1925, papers were signed consolidating the Curry Camp Company and Yosemite Park Company into the Yosemite Park and Curry Company. Donald Tresidder, son-in-law of Jenny Curry, was named president. The Board of Directors of YP&CCo. included such influential members as Harry Chandler, publisher of the *Los Angeles Times* and A.B.C. Dohrmann, head of a successful hotel supply business in the Bay Area. Part of the new agreement called for a year-round, modern hotel. It was time to select an architect.

Plans for a large, cohesive Yosemite Village in the valley required outside architects. Daniel Hull, NPS landscape engineer, introduced Mather to Gilbert Stanley Underwood, fresh from his graduate work at Harvard. In 1923, Underwood worked briefly for the NPS and submitted plans for a post office design for the village. It was soundly rejected. Yet something in Underwood's post office design, and his work at Zion (with Hull) impressed both Mather and YP&CCo. In July 1925, two months after Zion Lodge opened, the YP&CCo. Board of Directors hired Underwood. With the hotel site already selected by NPS and company officials, the thirty-five-year-old architect got his marching orders. Build a first-class, "fire-proof" hotel to blend with the environment.

Underwood had dreamed of creating a large rustic hotel in his work for the Union Pacific and its Utah Parks Company. While a much smaller version of the architect's Zion Lodge (downsized by Mather) was built in 1924, it was at Yosemite where Underwood, now with the support of Mather, created The Ahwahnee. Set in a meadow with the Royal Arches as a backdrop, and views of Half Dome, Glacier Point and Yosemite Falls, the hotel stands in relative isolation and remains today the most elegant and stunning hostelry in the National Park system.

Underwood began his grand plans with a projected opening of Christmas Day 1926. The idea was to have an "All-Year Hotel" built for the winter after the "All-Year Highway" (Highway 140) was completed. The highway opened July 31, 1926, The Ahwahnee on July 14, 1927. Ultimately, YP&CCo. would spend $1.5 million on the showpiece hotel.

The YP&CCo. Board of Directors hastily awarded the building contract to San Francisco contractor James L. McLaughlin. Instead of getting bids based on the architect's plans, the board, eager to begin construction, decided to forgo the bidding process—a decision all involved would regret. McLaughlin signed a contract to build the huge hotel in six months for a flat fee of $525,000. After McLaughlin signed on, 18,000 square feet were added to the plans—plans that continued to be revised. McLaughlin was furious, and the board responded in kind. April 14, 1927, minutes of the Executive Committee Meeting of the Yosemite Park and Curry Co. contain three courses of action concerning the "dispute over the Ahwahnee Hotel," ranging from dismissal of the contractor to a settlement. It was agreed that Donald Tresidder confer with McLaughlin and insist that the company "hastily complete the building" under the terms of the original contract, and upon completion of the building "an attempt would be made to settle all items in dispute." If he did not agree, McLaughlin was "to be informed to withdraw his forces from the building and to be informed that he would be sued for damages and all moneys in excess of the contract price."

Not only did the board feel McLaughlin Company was to blame, but "failure of the architect to provide satisfactory plans as rapidly as required," as noted in the minutes, added to the ongoing nightmare. A week prior to the hotel's opening, Tresidder again reported to the board that "much of the excess cost over the original estimates was due to the inefficiency and lack of knowledge on part of the architect." But the builder and architect were players in a serious game that included NPS, state and federal agencies. McLaughlin is credited with solving seemingly insurmountable transport and building problems, and The Ahwahnee is a testament to Underwood's talent.

As the bickering and finger pointing went on, an amazing building was being erected. Over two hundred workers, using horses to move boulders and state-of-the-art techniques to pour the concrete forms, forged on.

Built predominately of steel, granite and concrete, the building rises from the valley floor. It is an elegant yet rustic cluster of enormous blocks with two three-story wings. The core is six stories high, and each level in the asymmetrical design has a chimney, deck or porch protruding much like the rock formations of its setting. A hastily constructed porte-cochère, built ten days prior to the opening when it was discovered that the planned side entry would disturb guests housed above it, became the new entry. The true front of the building is on the opposite side. Hence, the campers and lodge guests who came in droves to the park were less likely to be put off by the hostelry so obviously created for the elite.

The goal of a "fire-proof" hotel was advanced, but not wholly achieved. Slate replaced the original shingle roof called for in Underwood's specifications, and only the roof framing in the Dining Room and the exterior balconies are wood—a marked departure from other Great Lodges. Instead of wood, Underwood called for siding and beams

Workmen use horses to move the huge boulders as the Dining Room takes shape.

Below: The putting green outside of The Ahwahnee, circa 1930s, was removed and the grounds restored.

made of concrete, both poured in molds formed to resemble timber, then stained to look like redwood. The effect is remarkable.

Finally, Mather had his grand hotel in Yosemite, and the YP&CCo., having spent a small fortune, had a showpiece for its operation. Knowing that The Ahwahnee would never be a "substantial earning unit for the company," they were nonetheless pleased to start promoting the hotel as the much-awaited all-year lodge ready to "cater to influential people who had ceased coming to Yosemite owing to the crowds."

Most in the valley lauded the hotel's architecture, but some, most notably "Mother Curry" and photographer and naturalist Ansel Adams, objected to its grandeur. Adams cryptically noted in his autobiography: "Yosemite's Ahwahnee Hotel…is a vast pile of steel and granite with huge concrete beams simulating timbers…the architect had tried to compete with the environment. He lost." Adams softened, however, even effused, when it came to the decor. Plans for a rugged "lodge" look were scrapped almost immediately, according to Adams, and Dr. Arthur Pope, a Persian arts expert, and his wife, Dr. Phyllis Ackerman, a tapestry authority, were commissioned to decorate and furnish the hotel. It was a brilliant selection. The two set about transforming the massive public spaces and one hundred guest rooms into lush, warm rooms in keeping with the board's desire that the hotel's atmosphere should be that of a "country home."

The team was acutely aware of just whose "country" the Yosemite Valley had belonged to. While their art history backgrounds were rooted in the Near and Middle East, the couple's interest was with indigenous peoples and the crafts they created. The couple turned to the motifs and pat-

terns found in the basketry of the California Indians as the basis of their entire design. Those patterns, found on the ceiling beams, stained glass windows, rubber mosaic tiles and multiple borders, reinforce the true roots of The Ahwahnee. Two of the most stunning examples are the five-by-six-foot stained-glass panels that top the huge vertical windows in the Great Lounge and the mural that fills the wall above the Elevator Lobby fireplace. Both were created by Jeannette Dyer Spencer, who was retained as resident designer when Pope and Ackerman left.

The stained-glass windows were not originally planned, rather included when the decorators found the floor-to-ceiling windows did not meet their specifications. Frantic, they turned to Spencer, a San Francisco artist, for a solution. Her geometric design not only reflects the valley light, but the Indian motifs painted on the beams that span the twenty-four-foot-high ceiling of the Great Lounge.

The cathedral-like Great Lounge is tempered by rich, warm golden walls, wood floors and richly upholstered furniture. Two enormous fireplaces of cut sandstone define each end of the room. The massive 17th-century English tables and most of the other furniture are original. The Gothic chandeliers are also original. Kilim, soumak and other Middle Eastern rugs were purchased in bulk and used on the floors and walls. The collection, recognized today as museum quality, is displayed on walls throughout The Ahwahnee.

The Great Lounge is the central focus of the main floor, but smaller spaces offer fascinating alternatives to the huge lounge. The first of these is the Main Lobby. Guests enter the lobby from the sugar-pine log porte-cochère. To the left is the Indian Room cocktail lounge, which was the original

Below: The Bracebridge Dinner is an Ahwahnee holiday tradition. Keith Walklet

Right: The Mural Room features Robert Boardman Howard's mural depicting the flora and fauna of the park.

Right: The Solarium at the south end of the Great Lounge offers a superb view of Glacier Point. A fountain of local Jasper rock with a balcony above are the only elements not meant for viewing the splendid Yosemite Valley.

Opposite: The 6,630-square-foot Dining Room is Underwood's nod to the lodge experience, with heavy log columns alternating with stone piers and sugar-pine roof trusses.

Right: The Ahwahnee's rough angles blend with the granite walls around it.

Below: Jeannette Dyer Spencer's mural above the fireplace in the Elevator Lobby uses swirling motifs from Indian basket designs.

porte-cochère. From this point guests can see Underwood's original introduction to the hotel: a long corridor with huge pillars, rubber mosaic tiles, floor-to-ceiling windows facing the meadow and a registration desk tucked to the right.

The Elevator Lobby, down the hall from the Main Lobby, is a buffer between the Great Lounge and Dining Room. Here, above the fireplace, is Spencer's famous basket mural. As described in a 1942 booklet on the hotel: " A swirl of painted basket patterns, [it] appears, bound together and balanced with bands that carry off their centrifugal force. Irregular silhouettes in black on red, taken from an old bead pattern, suggest by the direction of their lines the movements of the swinging doors on the one side and the sliding elevator doors on the other." The elevator door designs, now partially worn, are also by Spencer.

Past the Great Lounge are four more rooms. The Mural Room, originally the writing room, features the famous Robert Boardman Howard toile peinte mural. This nature study draws from the valley, with flowers, birds and animals, while the Winter Club Room is filled with park memorabilia. The Solarium, a half-circle banked with windows, and a simple fountain extend off the end of the building. The Stairway Lounge offers access to the mezzanine. Upstairs, one can gaze from the Tudor Lounge onto the Great Lounge. Two additional rooms flank the Tudor Lounge.

The natural elegance of Underwood's stone, concrete and glass interior is the perfect backdrop for the exquisite decor and artwork. The decorators complemented Underwood's massive elements with the smallest detail. The constant contrasts of large and small—huge pillars and fireplaces with delicate stencil work or massive spaces next to cozy sitting rooms and lounges—show that both the architect and decorators followed the natural surroundings where granite cliffs share the landscape with tiny wild flowers.

A bow to the traditional "lodge" feel of other National Park hotels is found only in the Dining Room. At some point, Tresidder and others considered changing the plan to a flat roof to accommodate a deck above. Happily, that was not the case. The 6,630-square-foot room has sugar-pine roof trusses—an Underwood trademark. The same pine logs line the north and south walls, but each has a steel core to help support the structure. Stone walls alternate with floor-to-ceiling windows. At the far end of the room is an alcove and another window offering up a view of one of Yosemite's great treasures—Yosemite Falls.

But construction of the Dining Room was difficult. Besides the halt in work to consider the deck, it was later discovered that the logs were shrinking and cracking. Eldridge "Ted" Spencer, who was the designer of the cottages that sur-

round The Ahwahnee and was also the husband of Jeannette Dyer Spencer, was called on to survey the situation. Besides dealing with the shrinking and cracking timber, settlement and displacement, Spencer noted with astonishment in a December 10, 1931, memorandum to Tresidder: "The blue print from Mr. Underwood's office covering the structural design of the roof shows that these purlins were to be supported on steel hangers. THESE HANGERS DO NOT EXIST." Additional consultants were called in and a solution of sorts finally found.

In this room one of The Ahwahnee's grandest traditions takes place. The Christmas Bracebridge Dinner is a five-night affair, with tickets offered on a lottery basis. The hugely popular event is part of the history of the hotel. A young Ansel Adams played the court jester in the early days; he and Jeannette Dyer Spencer soon ran the show. As historian, author and Bracebridge participant Shirley Sargent noted in her book *The Ahwahnee Hotel,*

Instead of wood, Underwood called for siding and beams made of concrete, both poured in molds formed to resemble timber, then stained to look like redwood. The effect is remarkable.

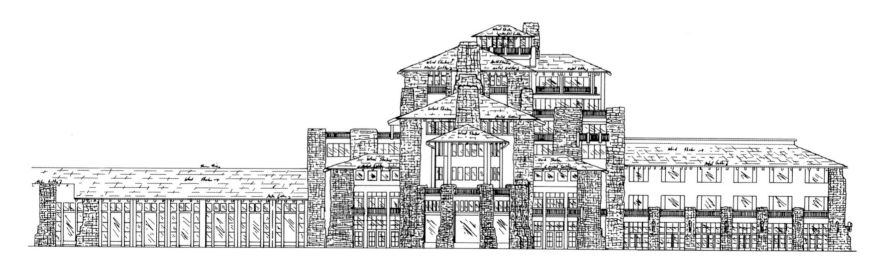

This redrawn version of Gilbert Stanley Underwood's south elevation plan illustrates the asymmetrical design with its strong vertical core.

"It was Adams who instilled the enchanting quality that still makes the Bracebridge unique and unforgettable." The feast, and all other meals are prepared in the 6,500-square-foot kitchen. Until the "federal government shutdown of 1995," only floods and World War II caused the cancellation of a Bracebridge Dinner.

World War II prompted the remarkable transformation of the elegant building into a military installation. On May 30, 1943, The Ahwahnee closed its doors as a civilian hotel, and on June 7, 1943, the U.S. Navy took charge of the hotel as a convalescent hospital. Most of the valuable furniture and artwork was inventoried and shipped to storage facilities in Oakland, California.

The commanding officers got the sixth-floor Tresidder suite, nurses occupied the fifth floor, and the Great Lounge was converted into a dormitory for 350 men. Other rooms and wings were used for wards, labs and X-ray machines. A humorous conversion was the El Dorado Diggin's bar (once in the mezzanine above the Dining Room) into a chapel. Temporary buildings filled the grounds and the Navy grappled with the best use of the hospital over its three-year occupation. The original plan to house neuropsychiatric patients was an immediate failure—the isolation added to the patients' problems. At times, up to 853 patients plus staff filled the hotel, cabins and surrounding buildings, and few were happy with the remote location of the Yosemite Valley.

When the Navy moved out, the Spencers and other staff returned and began an almost $400,000 restoration of the building and furnishings that included everything from fumigation to the reupholstering of furniture. Besides the building, the grounds, designed by Frederick Law Olmsted, Jr., were ruined. YP&CCo. later sued the government for damages.

Jeannette Dyer Spencer created the stained glass panels atop the Great Lounge windows, solving an "insurmountable" design problem perceived by the decorators.

The YP&CCo. was family controlled until 1969 when first Shasta Telecasting Corp. and then U.S. Natural Resources bought it. In 1973, MCA, Inc., bought the company; at that time The Ahwahnee was valued at $13 million. The MCA-owned

YP&CCo. undertook a major renovation of the hotel between 1975 and 1984. In 1993, after a competitive bidding process for a new concession contract, Delaware North Companies took over operation of the properties and changed the company name to Yosemite Concession Services Corporation (YCS). One of the conditions of the new fifteen-year contract to manage the properties included a plan whereby YCS relinquish its "possessory interest" in the buildings, in essence "donate" them to the U.S. government (an estimated value of $91 million by the end of the contract).

Over four million people visit Yosemite National Park each year. The approximately 90,000 guests who annually stay at The Ahwahnee—including royalty, dignitaries and celebrities—are part of its ongoing history. From the moment they walk past the reflecting pond, through the long entry and into the lobby, they are stepping into a world that was made of dreams and dissension. For all of the trauma of its construction, the criticism of its grandeur, it stands in perfect proportion to its setting, elegantly shaded by ponderosa pine, black oak and sequoia trees set against the majestic backdrop of granite walls.

Stephen Mather, who died on January 22, 1930, got his Great Lodge in Yosemite, his favorite National Park, and The Ahwahnee survives as Gilbert Stanley Underwood's most stunning example of rustic architecture in a National Park.

The Great Lounge features twenty-four-foot-high ceilings with floor-to-ceiling windows (each topped with stained glass), gothic chandeliers, and massive fireplaces. The color, design and decor give the room a warmth in spite of its size.

The Prince of Wales Hotel was Great Northern rail baron Louis Hill's final grand hostelry, giving him a landmark in the rival Canadian Pacific's territory.

A Whimsical Chalet

More than a decade passed before Louis Hill realized his dream of a third major hotel in the Rocky Mountains. He had long envisioned linking Glacier National Park to Waterton Lakes National Park in Alberta, Canada. Not only would a Canadian hotel complete his vision, but it would root the Great Northern Railway in territory dominated by the rival Canadian Pacific Railway. The CPR had successfully developed the Banff and Lake Louise resorts in 1887, and by 1902, CPR had a chain of resorts and chalets in Canada. These resorts were established before the Canadian park system, and rail lines ran through the landscape from the plains to the West Coast. Hill said his inspiration for chalets, hotels, roads and trails in Glacier National Park were European in nature, but more likely he got a lesson in development and marketing from his railway rivals to the north.

Hill picked the windswept knoll above Upper Waterton Lake in 1913, and first proposed the construction of a 300-room hotel. The setting was rivaled only by Glacier's Swiftcurrent Valley, but instead of the hotel hugging the shore of the lake, as with Many Glacier Hotel, the Canadian hotel would be perched high above the water's edge. The windy knoll at the foot of Mount Crandell offered both a pedestal for the structure and a vantage point offering guests a luxurious shelter from which to view the panorama.

The idea languished for a decade. During that time, World War I broke out; Canada, and then the United States, joined the war effort. In 1919, the Canadian government debated a proposal to dam the narrows between Upper and Middle Waterton Lakes. By 1921, the idea for a dam died, and Hill's

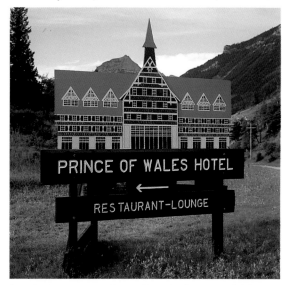

hotel plans were reborn. But the focus and drive that was the hallmark of Glacier National Park development had faded in fifteen years. Hill's focus not only wavered, but reached peaks and troughs as dramatic as the future hotel's surrounding landscape.

Hill was challenged by a new set of government and park regulations, and his gnawing fear

that visitors might never get to this little bit of wilderness was as real as the sometimes inaccessible roads to Waterton. Hill questioned whether to build the hotel at all, but finally gave the go-ahead after securing a land lease from the Canadian government in February 1926. Hill established the Canadian Rockies Hotel Company, Limited, and plans were announced that same month that indeed the Great Northern would build a 450-room hotel for $500,000. The announcement was made by Ralph Budd, president of the Great Northern Railway.

Thomas McMahon was commissioned to draw plans with the idea that this would be a replica of his design of Many Glacier Hotel. In May, Hill told McMahon to halt plans and withdrew funds for the hotel due to ongoing concerns about the roads. The next month everything was back on track, but McMahon was now behind schedule. In July 1926, Douglas Oland and James Scott of Oland Scott Construction of Cardston, Alberta, were contracted to build the hotel. Within days, they had a crew ready to work. Their deadline: July 1, 1927.

As Oland prepared the site, McMahon rushed on with the plans. Oland and Scott were accomplished builders, but the Prince of Wales project would be the biggest and most complex structure of the company's history. They had just completed

LOCATION: Waterton Lakes National Park, Alberta, Canada
OPENED: July 25, 1927
ARCHITECT: Thomas D. McMahon
HISTORIC DESIGNATION: National Historic Site, 1992.

105

the design and construction of a dance pavilion in Waterton. The railway knew the benefits of using a local contractor. Oland threw himself into the project, working sixteen hours a day. In his handwritten memoirs, Oland recounts his early problems with finding a reliable foreman, the lack of equipment and the deterioration of the dirt roads. "Another drawback was the lack of good equipment, especially hoisting equipment [for] all the many timbers used, and there were a lot, [they] were hoisted by horse power. There was no good excavating equipment to get south of Calgary and the soil where I dug the basement was all large boulders in clay." The rocks weighed from 100 to 400 pounds each.

While Oland's crew wrestled with the terrain, things were also rocky at Great Northern headquarters in St. Paul, Minnesota. Building had started late in the season, and while the foundation work was well underway by August, exactly what the completed hotel would be was undecided. Hill called in Toltz King and Day of St. Paul as consulting architects. As Hill and Max Toltz came up with more elaborate plans, Great Northern executives were thinking smaller. The proposed 300-room hotel plan was shrunk to sixty-five rooms. At the site, September rain had made the roads impassable by truck, and Oland was hauling freight by horse and wagon. Soon snow was falling. Framing began and the hotel took shape through October, but by the end of the month, Oland had laid off half his building crew. The railway's field accountant, George Anderegg, continued filing weekly reports. Timber, lumber, cement, shingles, brick and loads of other supplies were at the site. The plans were not.

If the bean counters at the Great Northern nixed Hill's plans to expand the site with additional

Upper Waterton Lake framed in the hotel's windows.

cottages and wings, Hill went in another direction. The Swiss chalet hotel plans grew—up. McMahon's original concept of a four-story structure was revised to a seven-story, whimsical dollhouse. Hill was in Europe touring France and Switzerland. When he saw something he liked, his photographer would take the picture and send it back to McMahon, and the architect would again change the plans. According to Oland's memoirs, "This meant that a lot of the structure as it now stands, had to be rebuilt four times, in early December I had walls and roof all framed, and this had to be torn down to the first floor." A fifth floor was added to the two wings that increased guest rooms from sixty-five to ninety, which necessitated the rebuilding of the dormers.

The hotel reinforced the Swiss chalet motif of the Great Northern's Glacier hotels, and at the same time attempted to defy nature by extending the knoll into an architectural landmark. Wind studies had been done on the site, but defiance of the one-hundred mph gusts was almost the hotel's downfall.

In December, building was going as planned and the hotel was taking shape. Built in sections, the two wings were enclosed and covered with scaffolding. On December 10, a storm blew into

By January 1927, two of the hotel's wings were in place after surviving a December windstorm.

Waterton. Workers battened down loose material; then the wind took over. According to Oland's memoirs, the resident engineer estimated readings of an average of eighty-four mph with gusts of one hundred mph. "I would not have been too greatly surprised if the whole building had blown down, as it was, it blew eight inches off plumb," wrote Oland. Timber landed two miles from the site. Oland's crew winched the structure back within four inches of its original spot. "After that I put a lot of extra bracing in that was not called for in the plans," he wrote.

Snowstorms, a second major windstorm and the deterioration of the existing roads plagued the project. When trucks couldn't deliver supplies, sleighs did the job. When even sleighs or horses couldn't get through the usual route, Scott found another road.

Oland became more determined to complete the job as close to deadline as possible. Crews steadily increased, from sixty in mid-January, to ninety by the end of February, and to 125 in April. When the Great Northern recommended postponing the opening until the 1928 season, it was Douglas Oland who objected. He wrote that if they would guarantee delivery of the material and quit changing the plans, he would "give them the hotel." By June 22, 225 men were on site, and the hotel was 91 percent complete, according to Anderegg's weekly report. On July 25, 1927, fifteen days after Oland and Scott predicted, the Prince of Wales Hotel opened. The cost was $300,000.

What had developed on the hill overlooking Waterton Lakes was the largest wood structure in Alberta, Canada. As with the Glacier hotels, the great timbers were transported by rail from the Pacific Northwest to Glacier Park Station, then moved by truck, horse or sleigh to the site. Had Hill bought the huge trees in Canada, the timber would have been transported by the rival Canadian Pacific Railway, which was *not* an option.

The hotel's core is the seven-story great hall lobby section flanked by two five-story wings and a single-story kitchen annex. The steeply-pitched gabled roofs are dotted with peaked dormers, and tiers of bracketed balconies cascade down the upper levels. A cupola and weather vane tops the "cuckoo clock" design. Balcony balustrades are jigsawn, and unlike the other Great Northern lodges, the huge timbers are all peeled and hand-planed. Originally, the cedar roof was meant to weather. It was painted in the 1950s and replaced in 1994 with a dark green, fireproof composite tile roof. The contrasting exterior paint emphasizes the structural detail. An extended second-floor balcony over the entrance offers shelter for arriving guests.

The exterior of the Prince of Wales Hotel seems like a fairy-tale creation, but it is also a shelter from which to view the park. Eighteen-foot-high windows along the lake-view side of the great hall frame a scene that none of Hill's artists hired to promote the hotels could possibly capture. Every window, from the attic to the cocktail lounge, contains the spectacular surroundings.

The great hall is far more refined than its Glacier counterparts. The architecture of the Canadian parks was rustic-Tudor, while to the south the rusticity reflected the "Wild West." The interior of Prince of Wales features the Tudor theme. The timber-framed lobby rises to a seventh-floor ceiling that serves as a crawl space. Access to the chandelier is from a small trap door in the ceiling, and for many years, the smallest bellman was lowered through the door to change bulbs and clean the fixture. The columns and trusses that fill the lobby

The tiny elevator is the oldest running elevator in Alberta. The hotel's historic designation is displayed next to it.

The Prince of Wales Hotel is perched on a knoll above Waterton Lakes in the spectacular Canadian Rocky Mountains.

The front doors of the Prince of Wales heralds the more formal chalet design of the hotel.

Below: Iron butterfly hinges and plates reinforce the joists.

The one-story dining room was always elegantly appointed. Windows flank the north wall, but the scene does not dominate the room. Wainscoting covers the lower walls with plasterboard above.

The guest rooms are charming, many with balconies and lovely views. The fifth- and sixth-floor rooms feature tiny alcoves, and access up narrow stairways gives the feeling of climbing into a very fancy tree house.

The original first floor of The Prince of Wales Hotel went through a number of changes, most made in the 1950s during the time the railway was renovating its hotels with hopes of selling. There was really no one to object. Louis Hill died in 1948, and with him the passion and understanding of his Glacier/Waterton developments.

While all of the hotels suffered from financial difficulties, the Prince of Wales' location with poor roads plagued it. As the economic problems compounded, an unusual alliance between the United States and Canada was growing. The International Rotary Clubs proposed to join Waterton and Glacier as an International Peace Park. In 1932, the peace park was dedicated. As symbolic as the park joining was, it could not stave off the effects of the Depression. In 1933, the railway did not open the hotel for the season. It would remain closed for two seasons during which time it suffered the ravages of neglect and weather. The closure was a blow to the town of Waterton and the Rotarians, but it pushed the completion of the Chief Mountain Highway linking Glacier National Park to Waterton Lakes Park. When the hotel reopened, visitors could more easily drive to the hotel.

The Prince of Wales Hotel was labeled early on as a haven for thirsty Americans made liquorless by Prohibition. A beer hall off the lobby became the

are all hand-hewn, and the wood is fitted and pegged together. Iron butterfly hinges and plates reinforce the joists. A second-floor balcony fills two sides of the lobby with jigsawn balustrades. Each floor has a balustrade balcony or windows from the stairs that lead to the upper-floor attic rooms.

Oland bid to build ninety bedroom suites and other furniture when his crew was bogged down by the weather or changes in plans. Instead, Hill selected most of the furnishing on a shopping trip to Winnipeg, but the decorating details reflected the real heritage of the area. Pictographs painted by the elders of the Blood Indian tribe filled the lobby. Hand-painted lanterns with the same Indian designs hung from the rafters.

first bar in Waterton. It was replaced by a gift shop in the 1950s. The Windsor Lounge was eventually added on the east side of the lobby, resulting in an unfortunate reworking of the once stately fireplace. The elegant double-sided stairway was partially enclosed, but the tiny elevator is the oldest running elevator in Alberta. The Indian pictographs were removed and some of the lanterns were moved to Lake McDonald Lodge and replaced by three-tiered aluminum chandeliers. Repairs to the timber columns have been made with care; all are hand-planed and honeycombed to replicate the original. The electrical system, fire escapes, sprinkler system, and kitchen were updated.

Prince of Wales Hotel was placed under the management of Donald Knutson of Minneapolis in 1957. In 1960, Donald Hummel acquired the Prince of Wales along with the Glacier Park hotels. Today, Glacier Park, Inc., a subsidiary of Viad Corp, owns and operates the hotel on land leased from Parks Canada.

Between 1993 and 1995, Glacier Park, Inc., redid the aforementioned roof, replaced the windows with thermal pane, and updated the bathrooms. In 1996, GPI revived earlier plans to expand the hotel. Any additions must be in keeping with the historic integrity of the Prince of Wales Hotel and be part of the total Waterton Lakes Framework for Managing Development Plan.

The Prince of Wales Hotel, whose namesake never saw the building, is a fitting final monument to Louis Hill. Not only does it defy logic and the amazing setting, but the exaggerated design immortalizes Hill's dramatic flair and determination.

The Prince of Wales Hotel's great hall, with its Tudor feel, is more formal than other Great Northern hostelries The original hand-painted Indian pictographs behind the desk and great hall lanterns were removed.

The Chateau, built into the gorge, seems to grow from the foundation.
Opposite: Oregon Caves Chateau is as much a part of the Monument as the cave itself. Jerry Barnes

Proving Less is More

By the mid-1920s, tucked in the Siskiyou Mountains in the southwestern portion of Oregon, a small complex of bark-covered buildings was taking shape. The site was one of the country's first National Monuments, and at that time, managed by the U.S. Forest Service. Unlike many of the lodges in western National Parks, the centerpiece structure, Oregon Caves Chateau, was not designed by an up-and-coming Los Angeles or Chicago architect. Gust Lium, an established local builder from nearby Grants Pass, designed and built what is considered a prime example of environmentally compatible, rustic architecture. By the mid-1930s, with changing economic times and tastes, the days of rustic architecture were numbered, and Oregon Caves Chateau is one of the last examples of a hotel built on public lands in the rustic picturesque style.

Interest in this woodsy niche of rugged land began deep inside the mountain, when in 1874, Elijah Davidson discovered a magnificent cave. The marble cavern became the destination for groups of adventurers ready to crawl into the bowels of the earth carrying burning boughs and candles to guide them, then breaking off stalactites and stalagmites to prove they had indeed been where few had ventured. Small outfitters and miners began taking out mineral claims around the cave and putting together expeditions to explore

them. Trails were cut and a cabin constructed. Around 1887, the Oregon Caves Improvement Co. was established, but financial setbacks, lack of title to the land and difficult access to the site tabled any grand development plans.

In 1906, the Siskiyou National Forest was established, and the land around the caves was withdrawn from mineral entry the following year. Soon after the first official survey of the area, on July 12, 1909, the 480-acre site was set aside as one of the country's first National Monuments. The proclamation read: "Any use of the land which interferes with its preservation or protection as a National Monument is hereby forbidden." It wasn't until 1922 when a road reached the cave

entrance area that any organized development took place. The U.S. Forest Service drafted plans for cottages, electrical lighting and steel ladders in the cave.

The following year, a group of Grants Pass businessmen secured a permit to provide guide services and build a resort. The Oregon Caves Resort (later named Oregon Caves Company) was made up of men with more than an eye on the dollar. They had a vision of what the cave development should be, and hired Arthur L. Peck to help develop the site plan. It was Peck, a faculty member of the Oregon Agricultural College, who envisioned a gable-roofed chalet near the cave entrance. And it was Peck who called for the Port Orford-cedar bark sheathing that would swathe all of the structures. The design was developed in concurrence with a U.S. Forest Service landscape plan. A trail and road system would connect the buildings, cave and view points in a natural landscape with structures that would appear as intrinsic extensions of the environment. The alpine village Peck envisioned is very much what visitors see today.

Like Crater Lake Lodge on the rim of Crater Lake and Old Faithful Inn at Old Faithful Geyser in Yellowstone, Oregon Caves Chateau is as much a part of the Monument's image as the cave itself. While the Chateau is now the centerpiece structure, it was the original Chalet and a number of

LOCATION: Oregon Caves National Monument, Oregon
OPENED: May 12, 1934
ARCHITECT: Gust Lium
HISTORIC DESIGNATION: National Historic Landmark, May 28, 1987

smaller buildings that first defined the architectural style. The architect of the original Chalet (which was replaced in 1942) is unknown, but the building featured Peck's design and material specification. A nursery, "Kiddy Kave," was completed in 1924.

When the Redwood Highway connecting Grants Pass with Crescent City, California, opened in 1926, seven guest cottages were added to the village. These cottages were designed by Gust Lium, who became synonymous with Oregon Caves architecture. Lium was the brother-in-law of Sam Baker, one of the founder's of the Oregon Caves Resort. Lium had an excellent reputation, and his private homes and commercial buildings reflected both his creative approach to architecture and his building expertise. Lium had already built two structures for Baker: one had long-span, bow-string roof trusses and the other was a marble-faced bank building in Grants Pass.

So, when Baker explained what the company wanted in the hotel, Lium knew just where to build it. Lium looked down into the ravine of Cave Creek Canyon. His inspiration may have come from the conifers in the surrounding forest, the vaulted caverns or the jutting gorge walls. His design was a Chateau that straddled the ravine, hugged the embankments and was topped with a steeply-pitched gable roof broken by shed and gable dormers, creating a roofline as jagged as a mountain range. The six-story, ten-sided lodge, covered in shaggy cedar bark and shingled in redwood shakes seems to have been dropped into the ground as a seedling. It simply sprouts up two stories from the roadway, seemingly part of the natural landscape, the lower four floors forming a root-like structure.

Baker accepted Lium's location recommendation, but a design review by the Forest Service was

required. Lium drew perspective views of the Chateau. According to Gust Lium's son, Robert Lium, his father normally drew floor plans, elevations, sections and unusual connection details. The original plans do not show the exact elevations, but they clearly indicate the variations of the three rectangular shapes that resulted in the ten-sided hotel. The two rectangular wings bank the sides of the canyon, with the conical center expanding as the building rises from the ravine. The original drawings show the front (east) and back (west) sides of the building appearing much the same size. When executed, the front of the building was much narrower, fitting neatly into the contours of the canyon.

Construction began in September 1931, delayed by the start of the Great Depression, and the Chateau opened in May 1934. Lium and a small crew of men created the building on a reinforced concrete foundation with post and beam interior supports. Most of the lumber came from the Grayback drainage, about eight miles from the Monument. The cedar-bark sheathing came from a railroad-tie cutting operation in the same area, and redwood was purchased from a regional supplier in California. Interior finishing woods, including ponderosa pine, madrone, white oak and Douglasfir were harvested locally. Native limestone and marble were quarried for the fireplace. Besides the building's fit into the shape of the canyon, the oversized beams and columns, matched with relatively normal joists, set the architectural pattern for the Chateau. It was constructed for $50,000.

The heartbeat of the building is on the first floor, deep in the ravine, where the furnace, sprinkler system and machine shop are housed. The second floor is storage and employee dining room. The third floor is the dining room, coffee shop and recently remodeled kitchen. Windows bank each end of the dining room and a conduit routes the cave stream through the dining room. Architectural historians point out that Lium's stream design came two years before Frank Lloyd Wright's acclaimed Fallingwater House at Bear Run, Pennsylvania. Look to the west, and the view is of the gorge, turn east and see the fish pond fed by waterfalls from the cave.

It is in the fourth-floor lobby, accessed from the main entrance off the parking lot, that the impact of Lium's genius unfolds. Unlike most of the lodges in this book, the Chateau's lobby is a single story. Instead of the eye immediately going up to a huge soaring space, visitors must first adjust to the low light, then take a long horizontal view of the room. Even with huge picture windows, the lobby has an aura as deep as the densely forested gully it straddles, as mysterious as the limestone and marble cave that was the reason for the lodge's very existence.

One must sit in front of the massive limestone and marble double-sided fireplace as the flames pop and flicker to fully appreciate the Chateau. Eyes adjust to the darkness of wood lighted only by firelight and the chandeliers, whose now-fragile parchment shades cast an amber glow to the huge lobby. Thirty-inch-thick peeled log posts, harvested from the nearby mountains, hold the massive beams. If you're lucky, "Bear" might be picking out a tune on the Welder baby grand piano as you survey the Fred Kiser art collection on the walls. The freestanding fireplace has a miniature cave on one side, with a stand holding a model caveman on the other hearth.

The golden aura is due in part to the wall treatments. The lower half is covered with redwood wainscoting and the upper portion made from "Nu-

The same chandelier design is in the dining room as the main lobby, but additional tiny wall sconces on the log support posts look like gnomes who have crept in from the wooded ravine.

Opposite, top: Oregon Caves Chateau framed by the mouth of the cave, 1936.

Opposite, below: Verandas ran along the back of the Chateau until they were condemned and removed in 1958 and replaced with catwalks and fire escapes.

Decorative wall sconces hang from log columns, right. A view of the pond, created by cave stream waters, is framed in the stairway window, below.

Opposite: The pond and Orford-cedar bark-covered Chateau.

Wood" pressed-fiberboard panels. The open stairwell is created from split oaks that rest on notched log stringers. Peeled madrone balustrades, polished to a rich mahogany glow, are topped with fir handrails and newel posts of lodgepole pine. As you ascend the stairway, you look out at the pond, falls and cave entrance. Follow the stairs down, and you are in the main dining room. It was here that a devastating flood and mud slide nearly destroyed the Chateau.

In 1964, a December flood forced mud and debris down through the archway at the Chalet and onto the Chateau. Men frantically broke windows and opened doors to let the mud slide pass through the building. When the flood of rocks, logs and silt stopped, the dining room—decorated for holiday guests—was filled with five feet of gravel and rock. Steps were ripped from the staircase, French doors torn from the hinges. The entire foundation had slipped. Gust Lium was brought in to direct workers to gently move the mammoth structure back in place. Lium, then in his late eighties, died months after the flood.

Most of the damage was in the lower three floors, but the original balustrades on the open stairway had to be replaced. The maple floor in the dining room was ruined and replaced with plywood subfloor and carpeting. African cherry paneling replaced the original wainscoting. The restoration left the dining room with its original ambiance.

The same chandelier design is in the dining room as the main lobby, but additional tiny wall sconces that look like gnomes who have crept in from the wooded ravine are on the log support posts.

The coffee shop is on the same floor. The original knotty pine paneling, birch and maple counters and stainless steel stools with bright red

vinyl seats line the soda fountain area. The oak
parquet floors in the coffee shop had to be removed after the flood.

Guest rooms in the Chateau are as varied as the
roofline. The original furnishings are still in most of
the rooms except on the first floor, where an unfortunate replacement of the Monterey pieces with
motel-like Mediterranean furniture took place in the
1970s. Colorful Pendleton blankets cover most of
the beds and every room has a view. The attic
rooms are pitched and offer special hideaways.

The story of the Monterey furniture that fills
the Chateau is historic in itself. The Mason Manu-
facturing Company, based in Los Angeles, created
the line between 1929 and 1943 under the Barker
Brothers' name "Monterey." The Mason Company
originally built its reputation on wrought iron lamps
and furniture. When the Monterey line debuted, the
"rancho" look was an immediate hit with the Beverly
Hills movie crowd, and the line's popularity grew.

The original Monterey furniture is reminiscent
of the Arts and Crafts Movement, but it was mar-
keted for a California audience. As the early brochure notes: "Although Monterey furniture goes
back to the early days of California for its inspiration, it is modern to the last degree in its comfort
and convenience. And the warm Spanish colors
add to the easy air of welcome."

The Oregon alder pieces have a textured,
antique look with rounded edges and distressed
finish. The drawer pulls, hinges and strap supports
are wrought iron, hand-forged at the plant by Max
Gebhardt. The floor lamps, andirons and wrought
iron accessories are also from the Mason Company
blacksmith shop. The wood is oil- or base-stained
then coated with a wax polish. The company also
devised a bleached wood, desert dust finish. Examples of both can be found at the Chateau. Many of

the pieces in the Chateau, particularly in the guest rooms, are hand-painted with wild flowers and desert scenes. Some of the chairs in the lobby have the branded horseshoe mark the company used for a short period.

George Mason, who was the sketch artist and draftsman for his father, recalled that the order for Oregon Caves Chateau was placed through the Meier Frank Department Store in Portland from the regular stock. Mason also confirmed that all of the lamps and wrought iron chandeliers were made at the Los Angeles plant.

The line was manufactured until 1943, when the founder, Frank Mason, died. George was drafted, and his mother and his father's partner sold the factory. Monterey furniture and accessories are highly collectible, and the pieces at the Chateau compile one of the largest original collections remaining at the site for which they were intended.

The furniture is one more detail that assures that the "alpine village" of Arthur Peck's vision and Gust Lium's execution, complemented by the landscape design of the U.S. Forest Service and NPS, seems so little changed from the era that the buildings took form. The "Kiddie Kave" nursery and cabins no longer exist, and the original Chalet was replaced in 1942. Gust Lium designed and built the three-story, asymmetrical Chalet with its steeply pitched-roof breezeway, the gathering point for cave tours. A ranger's residence, designed by Crater Lake National Park's resident landscape architect, Francis Lange, was built in 1935-36, nestled in the forest above the Chalet. The guide dormitory, built in 1927, was expanded in 1940 and 1972, and features peaked dormers. Unlike many parks, the additions are true to the origi-

nal vision.

With the exception of the removal of wood verandas from the Chateau (replaced with metal fire escapes) and repairs made after the flood, the Chateau remains the same. In 1929, retaining walls forming the Chalet courtyard and the fish pond below were built. The road system, parking areas, and trail system were all completed by 1935. The checking and comfort station, native rock walls

A guest room is filled with the original Monterey furniture.

and peeled log pole roadway lighting are all pre-1940. The integrated use of cedar-bark sheathing and native stone masonry set a precedent for state park and USFS architecture throughout the Siskiyou National Forest.

The National Park Service was into its "rustic" period when, under an Executive Order, it inherited administration of Camp Oregon Caves in 1933.

What it found was a project, originally mapped out by the Forest Service and local developers, in keeping with NPS philosophy. It was this striving for "harmony" between man-made structures and the environment that drove the rustic design philosophy of the time. At approximately the same time that the NPS took over, the Chateau opened and the Civilian Conservation Corps (CCC) set up camp at the confluence of Sucker and Grayback creeks eight miles west of the Monument. CCC projects gave the Park Service the necessary funds and manpower to plan for and execute a series of roads, trails and landscape work. The two ponds created from water diverted from Cave Creek and dry-laid, stonework built with rough cut limestone and marble from the cave, are CCC projects. At that time, the best and the brightest in the field of landscape design worked for the government, and the stone walls, steps and native flora plantings they designed have seasoned well.

Today, Oregon Caves Chateau (renamed "Lodge" in 1995) is managed by Oregon Caves Company, a subsidiary of The Estey Corporation. The building is owned by the National Park Service and Oregon Caves Company manages and maintains the lodge under NPS direction.

Oregon Caves development is a lesson in "less is more." This small canyon, cut into the Siskiyou Mountains by Cave Creek, accessed by a twenty-mile-long, winding two-lane road is unlike the panoramic settings of other Great Lodges. It is an introspective experience to stay at Oregon Caves Chateau. Here is a cocoon-like setting that pulls visitors into nature's fold, much like descending into the caverns.

The two-sided marble and limestone fireplace, dim lighting and the low ceiling give the lobby a warm, intimate flavor.

A conduit routes water from the cave stream through the dining room.

Monterey furniture fills the lodge. These chairs, left, are an excellent example of the style, now highly collectable. A Monterey writing desk, below, placed at the lobby window offers a view of the gorge.

Lower, left: Milk shakes are served at the soda fountain, which is complete with chrome stools with red vinyl seats.

121

Wildflowers surround Timberline Lodge with the Cascade Range seen beyond. Steve Terrill
Opposite: Telephone poles were carved into newel posts.

Timberline Lodge

A Stately WPA Legacy

Six miles up a winding road on Mount Hood, at the point where trees give way to volcanic ash, is the 74,000-square-foot Timberline Lodge. This huge, elegant piece of soft-gray architecture looks rather unimposing whether set against a surprise spring storm, buried in winter snow or surrounded by summer wild flowers. And it has always been that way, for there is little that can match the almost schizophrenic nature of Oregon's most popular peak.

Except, perhaps, the saga of Timberline Lodge.

Timberline Lodge is recognized as the first Works Progress Administration (WPA) project of its kind. A government built and owned hotel in a national forest, its purpose was twofold: to employ workers during the Great Depression and to advance tourism in the state. But it was not the first lodge on Mount Hood.

Mountaineers loved the moods of Mount Hood, and in 1889, a small lodge—Cloud Cap Inn designed by Portland architects W.A. Whidden and Ion Lewis—was built on the northern slope. In the 1920s, a group of Portland businessmen saw grander things, and began promoting a new hotel, but constant conflict over a lodge design and lack of financial backing plagued any progress. In 1935, backers formed the Mt. Hood Development Association; the same year, Emerson J. Griffith, a long-time advocate of a lodge on Mount Hood, was

named WPA Director for Oregon. With that, a link was formed for the much sought after funding for the development. Griffith quickly submitted an application to fund a recreation project, and on

December 17, 1935, the WPA approved it.

While the Great Depression was taking its toll on much of the nation, here on the slopes of Mount Hood, the New Deal administration of Franklin D. Roosevelt planned to put hundreds of men and women to work. They would build and furnish the first recreational facility on public land with predominately public funds. Griffith, with the support of Harry L. Hopkins, the WPA's first national administrator, threw himself into the

project. What originally had a price tag of less than a quarter-million dollars turned into a million-dollar experiment of not only public ownership of a recreational facility, but construction of a building that paid homage to the notion that the art of hand-crafted work linked to the region's pioneer past had a place in modern society.

In 1935, the U.S. Forest Service granted land use for the construction of the Lodge, now planned for the southern slope of Mt. Hood National Forest, an officially designated public recreation area. With $20,000 seed money raised by the Mt. Hood Development Association (in return for a promise that they could manage the Lodge) and funds secured by Congress, a design had to be agreed upon.

A trail of rejected lodge plans from the northern slope days paved the way for what would be a difficult process on the other side of the mountain. Weighing into the early design controversy was Frederick Law Olmsted, Jr., hired as a consultant by the U.S. Forest Service, who strongly objected to any modern "boxy...blocky" hotel plans. Olmsted was an original member of the Commission of Fine Arts, the agency the National Park Service and its director Stephen Mather regularly turned to for advice, and a strong proponent of architecture sensitive to its environment.

Emerson Griffith wanted John Yeon, a young architect from a well-established Portland family

LOCATION: Mt. Hood National Forest, Oregon
OPENED: February, 1938
ARCHITECTS: W.I. (Tim) Turner, supervising architect, Linn Forrest, Howard Gifford, Dean Wright, U.S. Forest Service
Gilbert Stanley Underwood, consulting architect, U.S. Treasury Department
HISTORIC DESIGNATION: National Historic Landmark, 1978

Above: The roof goes on the "head house."

Right: Stone masons hoist the rock facade in place.

Below: An early perspective drawing by Gilbert Stanley Underwood.

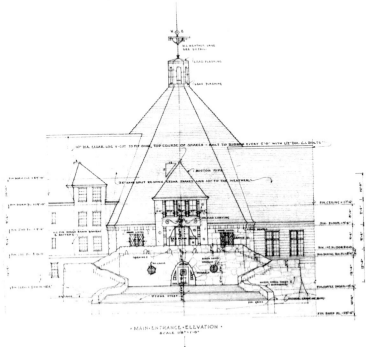

Architectural drawing illustrates the combined work of Gilbert Stanley Underwood and the U.S. Forest Service architects.

who had already made one rejected attempt on a Mount Hood hotel plan. Yeon's new low-slung concrete plan was also rejected, this time by the Mt. Hood Development Company, the Forest Service and the head of Oregon's American Institute of Architecture. The latter suggested a competition be held for the commission—the Forest Service was impatient. With the WPA application accepted, and still no plans, the situation was resembling the earlier Mount Hood hotel fiasco. The Forest Service needed a well-respected "name" architect who was familiar with wilderness construction and design. And while there was no love lost between the USFS and NPS, they turned to a proven commodity.

Gilbert Stanley Underwood, who was working as Consulting Architect for the U.S. Treasury Department in Washington, D.C., had left his mark at Yosemite, Bryce Canyon, Zion and Grand Canyon National Parks, and a personal friend of Stephen Mather, NPS Director, was recommended for the job.

It was Underwood's hope that he, through his private company, would be commissioned to design the Lodge. He was "officially" named consulting architect. While Underwood worked in Washington, Stanley S. Stonaker represented Underwood & Company in Los Angeles; it was Stonaker, not Underwood, who made the initial arrangements and took part in the planning meetings. While Underwood was working on the perspectives for a rustic lodge "of rough stones and timber, a sort of structure that will blend with the landscape rather than oppose it," apparently unknown to him, the Forest Service architects, with Tim Turner in charge, were drawing up their own plans.

In January of 1935, Underwood submitted his drawings in a variation of the rustic tradition he was known for. The plan called for three parts: an octagonal center lobby with a pointed "wigwam" roof oriented to the north with two wings. The center of the octagon would have a "great circular fireplace...high, massive columns...with heavy log rail shelters all of peeled log construction held together with heavy hand-wrought iron bands," according to descriptions submitted by Stonaker to the Forest Service.

Prior to receiving Underwood's plans, the Forest Service architects submitted four plans of their own; most consisted of a three-part design made of stone and timber with ridge and gable roofs in the stately picturesque style of a country estate. Griffith was pleased with Turner's plans and forwarded them on to Underwood. Underwood, although naturally favoring his more rustic and rugged design, graciously acknowledged the work of the Forest Service team that included Turner, Linn Forrest, Dean Wright and Howard Gifford.

Through the winter and into spring, plans were revised with Griffith weighing in with his opinions. In mid-February, Turner was summoned to Los Angeles to discuss the plans with Underwood. Week by week, the Forest Service architects took over the project. Ultimately, it was the Forest Service administrators growing loyalty to Turner and his physical presence in Portland that tipped the scales in his favor.

Linn Forrest, the younger university-trained architect of the group, did the elevation drawings as Turner negotiated on the design. Underwood's original concept of a core lobby with a steeply pitched "wigwam" roof was changed from an octagon to a hexagon and turned to the south following Forest Service recommendations. Instead of the "brutal" proportions Underwood desired, the Lodge took on a more elegant, spread-out design.

What evolved was a style most often called "Cascadian" after the range of mountains Mount Hood is part of. The more refined, alpine design not only reflected Turner's, Forrest's, and in lesser part, Underwood's tastes, but also the times and location. Instead of the rugged massive designs with the huge exterior logs of early Great Lodges, the shingled, board-and-batten, clapboard and stone exterior of Timberline paid homage to the existence of Portland just sixty miles away. Perhaps Underwood never fully understood that unlike Yosemite Valley, Bryce Canyon and the Grand Canyon, Mount Hood was a familiar sight to most who went there. Instead of offering the wilds of the relatively unknown West or Southwest to rail passengers, as was the case at Glacier, Yellowstone, Bryce and the Grand Canyon National Parks, Timberline Lodge was built for automobile travelers, mostly heading from the city for a quick mountain adventure. And while the Yosemite Valley, where The Ahwahnee stood, was more familiar to its public, it was not a scene urban dwellers could look at from the comfort of their living room window. Turner and Forrest, both knowledgeable and comfortable with the Northwest vernacular, drew from the classic country estates found in and around Portland.

Still, the Lodge holds true to the tenets of the NPS rustic architecture and Olmsted's premise that the building must blend with the landscape. Materials are indigenous to the region with timber and stone from Mt. Hood National Forest, and the subtle gray color blends with the volcanic ash soil and weathered trees that surround it.

As the architects hashed out the plans, the exact site of the Lodge had not been determined. In May, resident engineer Ward Gano and landscape architect Emmett Blanchfield were dispatched to make a new topographic survey. Finally, on June 13, 1936, construction began. Located at the foot of Palmer snowfield at the 6,000-foot elevation, the site offered a view of the Cascade Range, including Mount Jefferson, Three-Fingered Jack and Mount Washington to the south, and the Mount Hood summit out the back door. It was also situated to accommodate a ski area—the potential draw to make Timberline Lodge a financially successful venture.

Logistics and administration of the project were difficult, with federal, state and local officials trying to wrangle control of the project. A few crews set up camps in the winter; eventually almost 600 people worked on the project with a goal of nine WPA workers for every one non-WPA worker.

The three-story west wing went up, then the two-story east wing. The hexagonal "head house" was built between the wing spans. After the foundation was poured, rubble masonry and uncut boulders, quarried locally, were laid. The masons, many skilled Italian immigrants, worked into December laying the huge boulders and creating other stonework. As other alpine structures, Timberline has a steeply pitched roof covered with cedar shingles. The complex geometry of Timberline's roof adds to both the beauty and maintenance. The roofline is broken by a number of hipped and shed-roofed dormer windows. The roof of the "head house" protrudes above the other rooflines much as the summit of Mount Hood stands above the landscape. A 750-pound bronze weather vane tops the chimney on the "head house" roof.

Stone chimneys anchor each wing, where the rooflines dip nearly to ground level. In front of each chimney, tiers of shed-roofed dormers create

a formal cascade. These tier roofs are of copper to protect them from melting snow and ice damage. Copper has replaced shake on a number of the other roofs where the wood cannot withstand the beating of snow and ice.

As classic as the exterior seems, hand-carved rams' heads topping the fir columns framing the first-level entry and a thunderbird carved on the lintel above it are indications of what is inside. Walk through the massive, 1,800-pound, hand-hewn ponderosa-pine door, and the notion of architecture and art immediately comes together.

Naturally, the Forest Service architects and Underwood disagreed on the interior details. Underwood wanted a far more rustic look with peeled logs, stone piers and crudely carved decorative details using Indian motifs—details he thought could be economically achieved using WPA workers. Turner, with Howard Gifford doing most of the interior drawings, favored a more refined, finished look. The Forest Service won out. The "Timberline arch," a two-post and curved lintel design repeated throughout, came from Turner and Forrest. To Underwood, that sophistication represented "a little too much architecture" in the interior design. To the million tourists who come to the Lodge each year, it is an architectural backdrop for the hand-crafted details that *are* Timberline Lodge.

Underwood's two-entry concept to the "head house" was originally meant to separate hotel and recreational use. Skiers used the ground-level entry through an arched stone tunnel and pine door embellished with an Indian sculpture. Soon after the Lodge was built, an extension of the tunnel was added each winter to keep the snowdrifts from blocking the entry. Stone staircases curve up from the ground-floor level to the first-floor entrance.

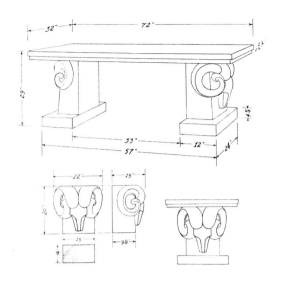

Inside, the ninety-two-foot-high hexagonal chimney rises from the lower-level lobby to the main lounge then through the ceiling. The chimney is actually six chimneys for six fireplaces: three in the lower-level lounge and three in the main lounge. While builders set the six pine timbers in symmetrical spokes around the hub of the chimney, and set six forty-foot pines into the six angles of the "head house," a design concept was unfolding.

Griffith, with recommendations from the architects, had decided that blacksmithing, wood-carving and weaving would complement the architecture. To achieve this, Griffith hired O.B. Dawson to supervise the blacksmith work and Ray Neufer to oversee the wooden appointments. But it was Margery Hoffman Smith, an interior decorator from Portland, who pulled the style of Timberline Lodge together.

Smith was brought aboard when Forest Service administrators decided the project needed a "woman's touch." She first toured the project with the "head house" complete and the wings in place. What was a temporary assignment turned into a four-year commitment. In her essay, "The Interior Design of Timberline Lodge," Smith described her experience: "My first visit to Timberline was with Mr. Griffith. As we walked through the half-fin-

The rams-head buffet table drawing, opposite, and as executed by WPA workers, above.

A thunderbird design is carved above the front door, which features cast bronze door knocker and wrought iron hardware.

Animal carvings fill Timberline Lodge.

shaped like woodchucks, rabbits and beaver), interior gates, light fixtures, chandeliers and fittings for the ceiling beams were created in Dawson's Portland blacksmith shop using hand-held tools at the forge and anvil. Lantern chandeliers were originally proposed by Forest Service architects, but Underwood wanted wrought iron, and Smith concurred—one of his few contributions to the interior. Underwood would not see the Lodge until October 25, 1936. According to *U.S. Forest Service Notes on the Progress of Timberline Lodge,* "Mr. Underwood expressed himself as generally pleased with the results to date and as far as could be ascertained, had little criticism to offer."

While the blacksmiths toiled, Ray Neufer's crew was busy doing woodwork for the Lodge in the basement of a Portland high school. The Lodge and furniture are of solid wood. The walls, beams, stairs, railings are made from fir, while the floors are of Oregon white oak. Other Oregon woods—red cedar, Port Orford cedar, Western juniper and hemlock—were also used. The six huge "head house" timber supports (ponderosa pine harvested in Washington state) were all hand-hewn with broad ax and adz. Newel post carvings of animals and birds were drawn, then workers turned utility poles into what are some of the Lodges most beloved pieces. The wood carvers followed Gifford's detail designs, Indian motifs (some taken from a Camp Fire Girls' Handbook) for the thunderbird carving over the main entrance and the Indian head on the ski lobby door. Other interior designs shown in Gifford's drawings were eliminated by Smith.

Smith, with the help of Dawson and Neufer, designed almost every piece of furniture. Time was crucial, and workers were dispatched to create pieces before blueprints were drawn. If a design worked, the plan was drawn and additional pieces

ished structure, I saw great possibilities. We could weave yards and yards of fabric for upholstery and curtains and bedspreads out of Oregon flax and wool, and put people to work building furniture which would carry out the simple large-scale feeling that Timberline conveyed even in its unfinished state. What an opportunity to use the work of fine artists to embellish the rooms!"

Griffith and Smith convinced WPA's Hopkins that the beautifully constructed Lodge needed furnishings to match. An initial $39,000 was allocated. Nearly two years later, $100,000 had been

spent. Eventually, the Fine Arts Division of the WPA provided money for the project. Even before funds had been found, Griffith had the architects adding detailed wood-carving and ironwork to their plans. In March 1936, using the wildlife and Indian and pioneer heritage of the region as her themes, Smith went to work.

The hand-forged wrought iron throughout Timberline is exquisite, from the coyote heads in the Cascade dining room gate to hinges, escutcheons and door knockers on the main door. Furniture fittings, window grilles, andirons (including some crafted. Even in the rush, the attention to detail and the overall impact of the furnishings as part of the architectural design are unmatched. In the hexagonal main lounge with its peaked ceiling and third-floor mezzanine, oak couches shaped in thirds, and hexagonal tables surround the massive fireplace and repeat the symmetry of the room. Even the shades on the lamps are six-sided.

The furniture reflects the bulk and size of the Lodge—there is nothing delicate about the raw-hide, wood and iron furnishing. But there is subtle-ty. Every curve and arch of a doorway or window frame is repeated, whether it is on the back of a chair or a chandelier. In her writings, Smith noted she was not happy with the curved-back design of the dining room chairs, but decided to repeat it "...and from the repetition gain a rhythm and pattern the single design does not possess."

That rhythm and pattern weave together as naturally as the hand-loomed fabrics Smith ordered. Weavers were recruited from the "white-collar projects" of Oregon's WPA. Eventually, about twenty women learned to work the looms and created nearly 1,000 yards of fabric for uphol-stery, drapes and bedspreads. Smith selected twen-ty-three different motifs such as Bachelor Button, Zigzag, Cornflower or Shooting Star for the forty-eight guest rooms. Appliqués made use of both an artistic vision and scraps of otherwise useless fabric leftover from clothing relief programs. Rugs were hooked from discarded Civilian Conservation Corps uniforms and blankets.

As practical as some craft projects were, the artwork was not only aesthetic but reflected both the region and the creation of the Lodge. "The Spring on the Mountain" mosaic, designed by Thomas Laman and Virginia Darcè; oil paintings by C.S. Price, one of Oregon's most distinguished

artists; two large panels depicting the builders of Timberline, painted by Howard Sewall; dozens of lithographs and watercolors all add to the living museum Timberline was to become. Douglas Lynch created a touch of whimsy with his incised lino-leum murals in the ski grill (now the multimedia Barlow Room). Each panel, now carefully restored, illustrates one of Mount Hood's seasons in the "Calendar of Mountain Sports."

Along the same lines are the murals and stained glass in the Blue Ox Bar. Apparently, Smith realized there was no bar in the Lodge design. A wood storage space was converted, and Portland artist Virginia Darcé designed the three panels and sign. The vivid fragments of opaque glass pieced into murals show the legendary Paul Bunyan and his blue ox, Babe, holding court in the tiny hide-away.

By August of 1937, President Roosevelt indi-cated that he would be willing to dedicate the Lodge during his trip to dedicate the Bonneville Dam. A frenzy of work ensued, and the wrought-iron gate to the dining room, the President's chair and a handful of guest rooms were completed. On September 28, 1937, the President dedicated Tim-berline Lodge in an address that was presented live over the radio. The President and Mrs. Roosevelt did not spend the night, but had lunch in the Cascade dining room to the delight of staff and workers.

The presidential dedication drained funds, and Turner in his log of October 14, 1937, was dis-mayed: "Due to the spending spree indulged in prior to the President's visit, there remains but some $6,000 for the completion of funds available. It is understood that $53,000.00 was expended within a three-week period immediately before the dedication."

While the Great Depression was taking its toll on much of the nation, the New Deal administration of Franklin D. Roosevelt planned to put hundreds of men and women to work here on the slopes of Mount Hood.

The chimney towers through the center of the main lounge of the "head house" filled with original furniture upholstered in hand-woven fabric, part of the ongoing restoration of the Lodge and its furnishings.

The Lodge didn't officially open until February 1938, and when completed, it offered three levels of lodging, from perfectly-appointed "fireplace rooms" to dormitories.

The Lodge's construction was both a WPA success and a failure. It was argued that for the amount of money spent not enough workers were employed and its purpose as a recreation destination was not in keeping with WPA principles. Others took a longer view of the completed Lodge, now considered an architectural masterpiece.

What is remarkable about Timberline Lodge is that so much of what was right, good and pure about the project still lives. But it wasn't always so. The Forest Service, responsible for operating the facility, could not give the promised lease to the Mt. Hood Development Company due to fears of conflict of interest. During the 1940s, the Lodge was operated by Timberline Lodge, Inc., whose members included men who had been part of the original vision. The Lodge was closed during World War II, but postwar skiers brought new popularity to the mountain. When the company decided to get out of the lodge operation business, so began its decline. The Lodge was ignored and mismanaged until it was almost too late. Just two decades after it was built, Timberline Lodge was closed for nonpayment of utility bills. Other managers tried again, and failed.

Enter Richard Kohnstamm, a twenty-nine-year-old Easterner with a master's degree in social work and a love of skiing. With no hotel management experience, but youth, optimism and family funds to get him going, Kohnstamm won the contract over 150 other applicants and reopened Timberline Lodge in December 1955. The first few years were financially challenging, but Kohnstamm upgraded skiing facilities, and the ski boom of the 1960s gave the new manager a much-needed boost. As business picked up and the crowds flooded the Lodge, the hand-crafted furniture, upholstery and drapes continued to take a beating. While Kohnstamm concentrated on the day-to-day operation of the complex's Lodge, restaurant, bars, gift shop and skiing, maintenance and structural problems, some guests with a sense of history arrived.

Blue Ox Bar walls covered with Paul Bunyan mosaic murals.

Rachael Griffin, former curator of the Portland Art Museum, "Gave us a lecture," recalled Kohnstamm. "She said, 'You don't know what you have there. You have something of world importance.' So we sat with our heads down and tails between our legs." When Griffin was finished, Kohnstamm understood that not only the building he fell in love with was worth saving, but so were its furnishings. Two things were obvious: the Timberline Lodge could no longer accommodate the growing crowds and additional money would be needed to expand.

Kohnstamm helped lobby, with the Forest Service's endorsement, for congressional funding that resulted in the 1972 construction of the 19,500-foot conference center. Two large C.S. Price murals were moved from the Portland Art Museum and Portland Auditorium to the new addition that now bears the artist's name. By the time the conference center opened, hopes were high that a day lodge would be next. In 1980-81, Wy'East Day Lodge was built. Timberline's ski lounge was remodeled, the front desk moved to ground level and the Rachael Griffin Historic Exhibition Center created in 1986.

What gave the restoration efforts of the Lodge a start was the formation of Friends of Timberline. In 1975, Kohnstamm and Portland businessman, John Mills founded the group and a twenty-nine-member board was organized. With the Lodge's proximity to Portland, people with power, talent and knowledge joined in. Their mission was to preserve and document the artifacts, furnishings, structure, historical significance and immediate environs of the Lodge and to raise funds and volunteers to accomplish their goals. And so it began.

Ironically, it was a government project that helped the Friends of Timberline start restoration. In the fall of 1975, ten CETA (Comprehensive Employment Training Act) employees began work on hand-hooking rugs, appliquéing and weaving fabric. Today, instead of dozens of themes for the guest rooms, there is a theme for each floor, and one for each of the eight fireplace rooms.

As the curator of Timberline Lodge and one of the 1970s weavers, Linny Adamson, explained, "We want to get the feel of the era, but acknowledge we're in the nineties. It is in the spirit of WPA." Because this is a "living museum" full of guests and tourists, furnishings must be replaced every five

CASCADE DINING ROOM

Wrought-iron gates with coyote heads, created by WPA workers under Orion B. Dawson, left, close off the Cascade dining room. The dining room, below, is furnished with the original tables and chairs. The chair backs feature a variation of the "Timberline Arch."

years. Between 1980 and 1990 one hundred new rugs were hand-hooked. The originals are on display. Five thousand yards of fabric have been hand-woven, and rawhide-laced chairs and lamp shades have been re-created, often by volunteers.

"We're on our third cycle, called 'Restoration of Restoration'," said Adamson. "The beat goes on. It's our tradition."

Timberline Lodge is a "Depression-era baby," and its management has evolved as a partnership among the government, nonprofit interests, and profit interests. The government-owned Lodge is managed by RLK Company under a special use term permit granted under the Granger-Thye Act of 1950. The Act allows the U.S. Forest Service to use the fees derived from RLK Company's gross revenues to maintain the historic Lodge and ancillary buildings under Forest Service guidelines. The nonprofit Friends of Timberline assists the Forest Service and RLK on restoration and replacement of the Lodge's priceless contents.

Together, they make possible the continuing saga of Timberline Lodge.

Epilogue

As I sat in the breezeway at Many Glacier Hotel, jotting down my impressions, a couple strolled by. The husband was recounting his days as a waiter at the hotel prior to World War II. "Heady days for a young man soon to be thrust into war," he was saying. "Wonderful days. Special days." As he pointed out the details of the lodge, he was reliving the past.

Back in my room, where the windows framed the perfection of Swiftcurrent Lake, I met the housekeeper, a college student from Texas. We exchanged our feelings about Many Glacier Hotel. She commented on how guests are sometimes disappointed that the rooms aren't more luxurious. "But I'm making up the beds, and I look out at the view of the lake and the mountains, and I weep because it is so beautiful," she said. "And *this* place is beautiful. I just stop and weep."

I felt the same emotions rise in me at some point during each stop at each lodge.

That's what is so important about preserving the Great Lodges of the West. They house not

Many Glacier Hotel is blessed by its breathtaking location and burdened by age.

only the political, social, and architectural history of our national past, but thousands of individual memories. Because the lodges are set in the most spectacular and best known public lands in the country, they can be lost in the difficult allocation of government funding. Buildings rarely seem as important as the natural wonders that encompass them, but the historic structures are an integral part of the park experience. There is a balance necessary to keep both the natural and cultural history alive.

Maintaining, restoring or renovating these lodges is a frighteningly expensive task. There are success stories like Timberline Lodge, Lake McDonald Lodge and Crater Lake Lodge. Lodges slated for demolition have been saved, others have had substantial renovations, while some have been damaged by thoughtless "improvements." It is never a one-time project to renovate a lodge; it is an ongoing task.

In the push and pull of government funding, concessionaire contracts, and public priorities, the buildings continue to age. We must help them grow old with the dignity they deserve.

Selected Bibliography and Sources

In preparing this book, I consulted a great many sources, far too many to list here. Historic Structure Reports, Preservation Architectural Guides, Resources Studies and Surveys, Furnishings Reports, National Register of Historic Places Inventory Nomination Forms, and Historic American Buildings Reports prepared for or by the Department of the Interior, National Park Service on individual parks and buildings were among those. Some are listed, but I am grateful to the authors and editors of all of them.

Adams, Ansel. *Ansel Adams, An Autobiography* (Boston, 1985).

Albright, Horace and Robert Cahn.*The Birth of the National Park Service: The Founding Years, 1913-33* (Salt Lake City, 1985).

Bartlett, Richard. *Yellowstone: A Wilderness Besieged* (Tucson, 1985).___ 1970 correspondence from Jane Reamer White to Richard Bartlett, courtesy of Richard Bartlett.

Buchholtz, C.W. *Man in Glacier* (West Glacier, MT, 1976).

D'Emillo, Sandra and Suzan Campbell. *Visions & Visionaries: The Art and Artists of the Santa Fe Railway* (Salt Lake City, 1991).

Djuff, Ray. *The Prince of Wales Hotel* (Alberta, CN, 1991).

Friends of Timberline. *Timberline Lodge, A Guided Tour* (Portland, 1991).

Grattan, Virginia L. *Mary Colter: Builder Upon the Red Earth* (Flagstaff, 1980).

Griffin, Rachael and Sarah Munro, eds. *Timberline Lodge* (Portland, 1978).

Haines, Aubrey L. *The Yellowstone Story: A History of Our First National Park.* 2 Vols (Boulder, 1977).

Harrison, Laura Soulliere. *Architecture in the Parks, National Historic Landmark Theme Study* (National Park Service, Washington, D.C., Nov. 1986).

Hughes, Donald, J. *In the House of Stone and Light* (Grand Canyon, 1991).

Hyde, Anne Farrar. *An American Vision: Far Western Landscape and National Culture, 1820-1920* (New York and London, 1990).

Juillerat, Lee. *Lodge of the Imagination: The Crater Lake Lodge Story* (Crater Lake, 1995).

Hubbard, Freeman. *Encyclopedia of North American Railroading: 150 Years of Railroading in the United States and Canada* (New York, 1981).

Kreisman, "Curtain Up." In *The Seattle Times/Post Intelligencer, Pacific.* May 6, 1990.

Leavengood, David. "The Mountain Architecture of R.C. Reamer." In *Mountain Gazette.* June 1976.

Matthews, Henry. "The Search for a Northwest Vernacular: Kirtland Cutter and the Rustic Picturesque 1888-1920" In *Art and the National Dream* (Irish Academic Press, 1993).___ "Kirtland Cutter: Spokane's Architect." In *Spokane the Inland Empire.* ed. David Stratton (Pullman, 1991).___*Kirtland Cutter* (Seattle, forthcoming).

Moylan, Bridget. *Glacier's Grandest* (Missoula, 1995).

Oland, Douglas. Personal memoirs, courtesy of the Oland family (Waterton, Alberta, Canada).

Rose, Judith, ed. *Timberline Lodge, A Love Story* (Portland, 1986).

Sargent, Shirley. *The Ahwahnee Hotel* (Santa Barbara, 1990).

Sceva, Paul H. *Recollections by the Old Man of the Mountain* (Self-published, 1974. On file, Mount Rainier National Park Library).

Tacoma Ledger: Articles on development at Mount Rainier National Park. Dec. 12, 1911; Dec. 17, 1911; June 27, 1915; Sept. 24, 1916, and *Tacoma Tribune*: Feb. 13, 1916, Sept. 14, 1916. (On file, Tacoma Public Library, Tacoma, WA, Northwest Collection).

Tweed, William; Laura E. Soulliere; Henry G. Law. *National Park Service Rustic Architecture: 1916-1942* (National Park Service, Western Regional Office, Feb. 1977).

Vaughan, Thomas, and Virginia Ferriday, eds. *Space, Style and Structure, Building in Northwest America,* 2 Vols. (Portland, 1974).

Weir, Jean B. *Timberline Lodge: A WPA Experiment in Architecture and Crafts,* 2 Vols. Ph.D. dissertation (University of Michigan, 1977).

Woodbury, Angus M. *A History of Southern Utah and Its National Park.* Utah Historical Quarterly, Vol. 12, No. 4, Oct. 1944.

Zaitlin, Joyce. *Gilbert Stanley Underwood, His Rustic, Art Deco, and Federal Architecture* (Malibu, 1989).

Bryce Canyon National Park Archives, Bryce Canyon, UT. Utah Parks Company contract, 1923; State of Utah and Utah Parks Company correspondence, Nov. 1923-Sept. 1928; UPC and BCNP correspondence, Sept. 1928-1968; Superintendent's Annual Reports, 1929-1942; *Partnership in Preservation,* 1988-89; active maintenance files; Scrattish, Nicholas. *Historic Resource Study: Bryce Canyon National Park* (NPS, Denver) 1985; Caywood, Janene and Grant, Frank. *Inventory and Evaluation of Historical Resources Within Bryce Canyon National Park* (HRS, Inc., Missoula, 1994); Union Pacific Railroad Archives, Omaha NB, correspondence and brochures collected by the Bryce Canyon Natural History Association (on microfiche); historical photos and blueprints.

Crater Lake National Park Archives and Library, Crater Lake, OR. Staehli, Alfred, AIA. *Crater Lake Lodge: Additional Notes On Its Architectural Significance and About the Architect*, prepared for The Historic Preservation League of Oregon, January 1988; *A Position Paper on Crater Lake Lodge, Crater Lake National Park,* The Historic Preservation League of Oregon, August 1986; Robert Lium, personal memoirs; National Park Service, Fletcher Farr Ayotte, Architects, CH2MHill, Consulting Engineers; *Rehabilitation of Historic Crater Lake Lodge, Comprehensive Design Program, Historic Character/Documentation.* March 30, 1990; Mark, Stephen R., *Administrative History,* Ch.17, *Planning and Development at Rim Village, Crater Lake National Park* (NPS, Seattle) 1991.___ *Historic American Buildings Survey, Oregon Caves Chateau,* HABS. OR-145, (NPS, Denver) 1989; historical photos (Crater Lake Lodge and Oregon Caves Chateau).

Federal Records Center, Sand Point, WA. Mount Rainier National Park Superintendent's reports and correspondence, 1915-1919.

Friends of Timberline, Portland, OR. Correspondence, Presidential dedication visit to Mt. Hood; *The Interior Design of Timberline Lodge,* by Margery Hoffman Smith, undated; historical photos and blueprints.

Glacier National Park Archives and Library, West Glacier, MT. Glacier National Park superintendent's annual and monthly reports, 1911-14; Glacier Park Hotel Co. Bulletin #4, July 15, 1914; Correspondence files, 1911-16; Great Northern Railway promotional brochures; McDonald, James. *Historic Preservation Architectural Guide, Lake McDonald Lodge, Glacier National Park* (NPS, Denver) 1984, revised 1985.___ *Many Glacier Hotel, Glacier National Park, Architectural Preservation Guide* (NPS, Denver) 1984; historical photos and blueprints.

Grand Canyon National Park Library and Archives, Grand Canyon, AZ. History file, El Tovar: *A New Hotel at the Grand Canyon of Arizona,* 1909; *Hotel El Tovar,* 1905; *Titan of the Chasms, The Grand Canyon of Arizona,* 1904; *Doing the Grand Canyon,* 1909; Correspondence, Atchinson, Topeka & Santa Fe, 1902-11; *Arizona Daily Sun ,* April 1, 1975, Sept. 8, 1975, Nov. 1, 1981; Superintendent's Annual Reports, 1926-28, 1932, 1936; Grand Canyon Lodge, North Rim file, *The Hotel in the Wilderness,* author unknown; UP Railroad promotional brochures, 1928-32. History file, Fred Harvey Company: *The Fred Harvey Collection: 1889-1963*; AmFac, Inc. press release, July 10, 1968. Historical photos.

Minnesota Historical Society, St. Paul, MN. Great Northern Railway, Presidents file, 6482, 6483, 6497, 6500, 6741 and 132.F.2.2F, 133.1.8.11B, 137.C.6F , Great Northern Railway Co. Records; Glacier Park Division, "Old Subject Files," Glacier Park Co., 132.F.16.10; Glacier Park Co., Canadian Div., 132.F.19.5(B); historical photos.

Mt. Hood National Forest, Zig Zag Ranger Station, OR. Linn Forrest, oral history, 1978; *Some Timberline Lodge Recollections,* by Ward Gano, July, 21, 1978; Report on Forest Service Activities in Connection with the Visit of the President's Party to Mt. Hood National Forest, Sept. 28, 1937; U.S. Forest Service Notes on the Progress of Timberline Lodge, Mt. Hood; Frederick Olmsted, Jr. letters, Feb. 18, 1931, March 14, 1931 (design file); Fulton, Eleanor. *Historic American Buildings Survey, Timberline Lodge.* (HABS OR-161,1995); historical photos and blueprints.

Mount Rainier National Park, Tahoma Woods and Longmire, WA. Allaback, Sarah. *The Rustic Furnishings of Mount Rainier National Park, 1916-1966.* (HABS, Sept. 1996); Snow, David. *Historic Structure Report, Mount Rainier, Paradise Inn,* (NPS, Denver) 1978; historical photos.

Oregon Caves National Monument, Oregon Caves, OR. Interpretation Division Files, *General Data, History of Oregon Caves National Monument, 1849-1989*; History Files, correspondence, 1922, 1923, 1931, 1929, 1936, 1964-65; *Grants Pass Courier and San Francisco Examiner,* misc. articles.

Technical Information Center, National Park Service, Denver Service Center, Denver, CO Copies of architectural drawings and blueprints.

Yellowstone National Park Archives, Mammoth, WY. Box C-14, file 332.2, YPHCo., 1925-27; YPC-14, lodges and camps, 1932-37; YPC-34, business correspondence, 1934-36; YPC-126, Old Faithful Inn, 1959; Letter box #39, file #10, accommodations at hotels and camps; Superintendent (or Acting) Annual Reports 1890, 1899, 1901 and 1904; *Through Wonderland,* Northern Pacific Railway brochure, 1905; YPC, Volume 3 (furniture) Inventory, Sept. 30, 1929, The American Appraisal Co.; Clemensen, A. Berle. *Historic Structure Report, Old Faithful Inn, Yellowstone National Park* (NPS, Denver) 1982; historical photos.

Yosemite National Park Research Library and Records Center, Yosemite, CA. Spencer, Jeannette Dyer, *Ahwahnee, Yosemite National Park, California,* The Yosemite Park & Curry, 1942, #11130; Underwood, Gilbert Stanley, *Specification for the Ahwahnee Hotel; Ahwahnee— Yosemite's New Hotel, National Motor,* August, 1927, Box #79; *History of the United States Naval Special Hospital, Yosemite National Park,* Yosemite Park & Curry Co., Jan. 15, 1946; Correspondence and memos, Box #79; the Ahwahnee Hotel file; YPCC minutes of Board of Directors, Box #8; historical photos.

Zion National Park Archives, UT. Superintendent's Annual Reports, 1928-32.

Index

Italic numerals indicate illustrations

Photograph and Illustration Credits

Color Photography

Fred Pflughoft & David Morris, pages: Back book jacket, 1, 14, 15, 17 (right), 18, 19, 27, 29, 31, 45, 46, 53 (top), 55, 63 (top left & bottom), 64, 65, 72, 74, 75, 77, 82, 84, 88, 98 (top), 99, 100 (bottom), 103, 111, 116, 118, 119, 120, 121, 123, 127, 128, 130, 131, 136

David Morris, pages: Cover (The Ahwahnee), 4-5, 21, 23, 33, 35, 49, 52, 53 (bottom), 69, 73, 79, 83, 85 (top), 87 (top), 91, 98 (bottom), 100 (top), 102, 105, 107, 110, 112, 117, 132

Fred Pflughoft, pages: Cover, (El Tovar), 2-3, 11, 17 (left), 22, 30, 32, 36-37, 40, 41, 44, 47, 48, 56, 57, 60, 66-67, 68, 78, 85 (bottom), 90, 104, 108-109

Jerry Barnes, page 113

Jeff & Alexa Henry, pages: 10, 89

Steve Terrill, page 122

Keith Walklet, pages: 93, 96-97, 98 (left)

Historic Photos & Drawings

Pages: 6, reprinted with permission Friends of Timberline Lodge (1996); 8, Yellowstone National Park, YELL#31381; 12 & 13, Montana Historical Society Library; 16, Yellowstone National Park, J.E. Haynes, YELL#31398; 24 (bottom), Dept. of the Interior, National Park Service, Denver Service Center, #70332;* 24 (top) Grand Canyon National Park, #9453; 25, Grand Canyon National Park, #9852; 28 Grand Canyon National Park, #9837 (left), #99857 (right), #9835 (bottom); 34 (right) Glacier Natural History Association, Hileman 1062, HPF 1397; 34 (bottom) Bob Jacobs collection; 39, Glacier Park, Inc.; 42, Eastern Washington State Historical Society, L84-207.226; 43 (top) Glacier Natural History Association, Hileman, 8017; 43 (lower right) Glacier National Park, Marble, HPF 8198; 50, Glacier Natural History Association, Hileman 4222, HPF 2219; 51 (top) Minnesota Historical Society, 132.D.19.10(F), file F4; 51 (bottom) Eastern Washington State Historical Society, L84-207.6; 54 Glacier Natural History Association, Hileman 4161; 58 (top) Crater Lake National Park, #25573; 58 (bottom) Photo courtesy Klamath County Museum; 59 (top) courtesy Parkhurst family; 59 (bottom) Oregon Historical Society, Oi #C-22; 62, Crater Lake National Park, Earl Russell Bush #268H; 63 (top right) Crater Lake National Park, Earl Russell Bush #4701; 70 (top) Mount Rainier National Park Collection #4543; 70 (bottom) Dept. of the Interior, National Park Service, Denver Service Center; 71, Mount Rainier National Park Collection #909; 80, Union Pacific Museum Collection; 81 (bottom) Bryce Canyon National Park #1289, 81 (top) ACC 368 CAT 3892; 87 (below) Union Pacific Museum Collection, Grand Canyon Natioanl Park #8146; 92 (top) The Yosemite Museum, National Park Service, JV Lloyd #65892, 92 (bottom) #RL-6788; 95 (top) The Yosemite Museum, National Park Service #RL-15,382; 95 (bottom) Yosemite Concessions Services Corp.; 101, Dept. of the Interior, National Park Service, Denver Service Center;* 106 (bottom) Great Northern Rwy. Co. Records, 132.F.19.5 (B) 22/F/12/2F, Canadian Div. Subject Files, Minnesota Historical Society; 106 (top) Glacier Natural History Association, Hileman 6514; 114 (top) Crater lake National Park, OrHi 84547, Caves Co., Sawyers 16-353; 114 (bottom) Oregon Caves Co.; 124, Reprinted with permission of Friends of Timberline (1996); 126, USFS collection;.

* Redrawn by Linda McCray from damaged historical documents

The Prince of Wales is an elegant site from which to view the splendor of Waterton Lakes National Park, Alberta, Canada.